PRAISE FOR

SAFER THAN THE KNOWN WAY

"Contemporary debates around the question of God almost exclusively take place in the field of affirmation or negation. God exists, or God does not exist. With the most reasonable position often appearing in the guise of agnosticism. However, the most perceptive thinkers of religion have long since left this barren plot of land, seeing in the signifier 'God' a naming of that which is otherwise than being. In *Safer than the Known Way*, Maria French powerfully weaves together her personal story with deconstructive theory to entice the reader beyond that infertile field, into a rich world full of new horizons, new hopes and new (im)possibilities."

Peter Rollins, theologian and author of "The Idolatry of God" and "The Divine Magician"

"A reverent provocateur, Maria breaks all the rules but manages only to prod and never poke. Refreshingly unbiased, her agenda is there shouldn't be one. Maria writes with an informed fortitude—academically and personally earned; yet, she manages within that strength to both offer up and invite vulnerability. An invitation to what she calls a "disruptive peace." Maria is always showing up for herself, both past and future, and emboldens the reader to have this same courage. All the while maintaining a surprisingly grounded-in-the-moment reflective tone. She crafts stunning prose that immerses the reader movingly in her most soul-altering memories. A memoir wrapped in a useful curriculum, Maria presents an integrative historical and theological narrative, but easily connects with readers who, like her, are on some level fond of the Christian clichés of their formative years—simply put, she knows her stuff and she knows you. She holds a relentless faith in faith, and an inspiring optimism in the toiling; she sits in awe of it. A religious memoir with surprising scope and depth, but with a glaring lack of anything to prove. In her readers' questioning, she offers companionship. So go, have a cry in the chapel. And take this book with you. She won't tell you what your relationship with Christianity should be, but she'll help you eulogize it and wait with you while a path forms. She'll wonder with you what undiscoverable "other" might lie on the other side. After all, it's safer there."

Kim Stewart, licensed psychologist and religious trauma expert

"Maria Francesca French has penned an inspirational spiritual adventure just right for our time of constant white water. This text reflects the wisdom of Solvitur Ambulando, "it will be found in the walking," in which the journey itself is, as Nelle Morton asserts, home! Home is adventurous, on the move, alive, and constantly changing. Maria bids us to be comfortable with change and transformation, even when these uncomfortable changes involve letting go of "certainties" of faith and images of God. With the author of Lamentations, Maria reminds us that faith is new every morning. In the novelty of what is to be, the becoming of what is, and the transformation of what was, we experience abundant life. This book, even when it describes tears shed, is a celebration of life in all its Wondrous Beauty and Mystery. In walking with Maria Francesca French, you may find a faith without fences and foundations, and grace and gratitude without certainty. Rejoice, be amazed, and delight in the wonder of all being."

Bruce Epperly, professor and author of "The Elephant is Running"

"This is a gorgeous and original book. A tour de force weaving together personal, philosophical and theological strands, this is a book that brings the reader into confrontation with the most fundamental questions about God and what it means to believe (or not). Always doubting, always warm and always provoking, *Safer than The Known Way* is a thrilling and moving journey of faith."

Victoria Brooks, writer, researcher, and author of "Fucking Law" and
"Mistress Ethics"

"This visionary book is a carefully constructed piece of work, a labour of love and a narrative of someone who is deeply searching for new ways of speaking of the unspeakable. It is an oeuvre informed by the philosophy of Jacques Derrida, John Caputo, Mark C. Taylor and others. *Safer than the Known Way* restores a place of belonging to those that have stepped onto a new path to encounter what is tout autre - wholly other - and asks us to engage something that requires us to step away from the safe binaries we might be used to."

Bea Mariam Killguss, educator and existential coach

"Maria Francesca French holds space for those who question their faith and the rules they've been brought up with. *Safer than The Known Way* addresses the buzz word, "Deconstruction," giving evolving Christians a safe place to go beyond liturgical and cultural traditions. Through personal stories and extensive theological study, Maria French encourages people on their journey to or from (little g) god or (Big G) God."

TC Newman, television and digital journalist

SAFER THAN THE KNOWN WAY

A POST-CHRISTIAN JOURNEY

MARIA FRANCESCA FRENCH

Copyright © 2023 by Maria Francesca French, First Edition

[Scripture quotations are from] New Revised Standard Version Bible, copyright © 1989 National Council of the Churches of Christ in the United States of America. Used by permission. All rights reserved worldwide.

Cover by Rafael Polendo
Interior layout by Matthew J. Distefano
ISBN 978-1-957007-41-0
This volume is printed on acid free paper and meets ANSI Z39.48 standards. Printed in the United States of America

 QUOIR

Published by Quoir
Chico, California
www.quoir.com

For Barry, a beautiful human, brilliant mind, and tender heart.
You are so loved.

CONTENTS

FOREWORD

The songwriter Tom Waits once likened the process of writing to a conjuring trick—a particular kind of magical performance, in which the magician has summoned something, seemingly out of thin air. If writing is a like conjuring trick, the magic doesn't come out of nowhere, but from the threads of information, ideas, and opinions which are coupled with the hopes, desires and bravery of the writer to produce the magic. I say bravery because there is a bravery required to writing-to face the blank page, to committing ideas to paper, to letting the writing find its own path.

I also say bravery because I have been lucky enough to see Maria bravely come into her own; fight to discover her own voice; wrestle her way out of straitjackets, both personal and theological, and make her way in life with a new found courage that finally matches the curiosity she has always possessed.

The book you hold in your hands is a prime example of both her voice, and her bravery. It's never easy to lay out one's own ideas for the world to pore over, critique, and agree or disagree with, nor is it easy to challenge conventional wisdom, or ideological dogma, with poetic visions of other ways of seeing the world, particularly when the world one addresses is of the theo-religious kind, but that is what she has done.

This is a book for all who must be brave, who perhaps like her, have straitjackets to wriggle out of, skins to shed, dogmas to reject and futures to explore. It is a book which tells a personal story of familiar struggles that many who have grown up bathed in a particular kind of religiosity have experienced—a form of faith that for many no longer feels fit for purpose. It's also an account of the ways in which she has personally wrestled with things, and the new ideas that have helped her not only overcome the past, but also to find a different path forward.

The safe way, is a way of pavements, of clear direction, well-trodden and comfortable. When you turn from that way you might find your-self at a crossroads, one which the writer Frédéric Gros, says, "shimmers like hesitant stars," where you can, "rediscover the tremulous fear of choosing, a vertiginous freedom," this is the way this book wants to take you, it's safer than the known way.

— **Barry Taylor**

ACKNOWLEDGMENTS

There are so many people who I feel I need to thank. As this book reads both as a spiritual memoir and perhaps a theological manifesto, I didn't get here all on my own. As you read these pages, you will see all of the thinkers and theologians who warrant my undying gratitude. It will be impossible to name everyone both known and unknown, living and dead, who have led me here. But it must be said, we stand on the shoulders of all who have helped write our story.

I want to first thank my husband, Simon Mitchell. This book would not have been possible without the time and space our life together in England gifts me. Your love, companionship, the mutuality we offer each other, the safe haven our relationship is, and your unwavering commitment to my work have fed my own passions and been a sustaining factor in the writing of this book. You also meticulously edited the manuscript and for this I am so grateful. It has no more loving and encouraging hands than yours.

Sadie Cullumber and Beth Hutton, as you have understood the task cathedral ruins offers us and invites us into. Women I can run with like wolves who aren't afraid of the future, and, more importantly, the present. These women have been my confidents and closest friends during so much of the work I speak about here, as well as my own growth and transformation. I am indebted.

The Bridge Girls—Andy Halverson, Rachel Bundy, Annie Lyle, Kati Dean, and Christina Smith. I take you with me wherever I am, wherever I go. My first wild women, the archetype that gave me strength, courage, and bravery for the journey ahead. Support during so much change and an immovable undergirding for the risk required in the kind of lives we lead. Thank you. I will love you forever, I already have.

Bea Mariam Killguss, you came almost out of nowhere. And as each stage of my life has been so gracious and generous offering up the best of a new female friendship, you have been an unexpected but most welcome gift. Our weekly, standing, pandemic zooms, England calling Australia and now England calling France, was no small mercy. You have been a beautiful miracle in my life and many of our conversations allowed me to flesh out some of the thought represented here. Thank you for being so supportive and one of my biggest cheerleaders throughout this book writing process.

My mom Jennifer Troccoli Esposito and my dad John Esposito. My Italian heritage, my fiery blood, springboards of my life. I know the story I tell is the best of both of you. I know the underlying river that flows throughout my life, flowed from you first. For this I am proud and thankful. Mom, thank you for you for you lifelong commitment to your pursuit of faith. Dad, thank you for your unsinkable nature.

For my aunt, Kathleen Troccoli, who has been a consistent and formidable presence in my life my whole life. Who helped introduce me to Jesus and gave me an imagination for a different kind of life. This is what started it all. You showed me life and what it means to really live it. And I'm not sure I would have had the bravery, if you weren't brave first.

Sandrine Adeline, what can I say? How can I thank you for our life together in France? It changed me. It changed my life and its trajectory. What do I believe? Well, I believe in magic. Because of you.

My best friend, Barry Taylor. Thank you for toiling with me all these years. You pulled me forward, past the shadows, past the Light, and gave me vision for all that would become *safer than the known way*. No words but these...thank you from the bottom of my heart.

PREFACE

I'm just someone who has lived to tell.

But I'm not telling you a story of atheism in the wake of a most disappointing and unimaginative, unkind and unreasonable, worship-obsessed God. I'm not telling you a story of a God who is socialist and reconciling; one who denies love, inclusion, and community to no one.

Others have told those stories. Others have written those books. That is not what you will read here. I've woven my story of discovery throughout these pages, but we will go on a journey together. It will seek to move past discussions of god as wrathful judge or peace-loving hippie. It is a conversation that will move from a world of certainty and knowledge to one that survives, thrives, and writhes in uncertainty and unknowability. It is the discussion after we leave traditional notions of belief and Christianity in our dust but still deeply desire to engage our faith, everything it means to us, and the story we started writing so long ago.

We are about to embark on a discourse of what it means to be post-Christianity, post-belief, post-church, post-God, but still engage god. Yet not in any way familiar, as we find ourselves at home in the presence of such a specter. This specter we see running itself in, out, and through our narratives up until now. The specter comes to haunt and taunt, but the difference is perhaps now we have ears to hear. This is not a book about parlaying one brand of belief into another, or exchanging one God construct for another. It's about smashing all paradigms we might have ever had for this sort of thing and finally paying heed to those pesky, undeniable, and enchanting whispers that come for us again and again.

The post-Christian conversation does not speak of god in ways that are ontological, teleological, metaphysical, supernatural, or transcendental. This is not to say those realities are objectively denied. However, it is simply not what we are after or, better yet, not the point. So, we are not going to speak of god in ways that denote being, consciousness, agency, or interventionism. So, what is left? Are we to speak of god as metaphor, allegory, myth, drug, palliative, in other words, not real? Are those our choices? Either the big God who lives in the sky or a fairy tale? Can we not do better than that? Can we not engage our faith in any real, meaningful, and transformative way outside of these two paradigms? Can we talk about god and the things of god in ways that matter for our life, our ethics and ethos, and how we make meaning that doesn't ask us to sacrifice our stories; our journeys?

This book doesn't claim to answer questions, it brings you a new conversation. One that lifts us from the one-dimensional belief in a God or not-God. One that moves past traditional notions of theism, while simultaneously saying atheism isn't near good enough. One that eclipses the decades-old debate between conservative and liberal Christians, about who got it right.

ᵢing to talk about god, there has to be more than this. Not
ᵢ offer an answer to all our questions, conundrums, and
curiosities, but in ways that invite into all that is unknown, uncertain,
ungrasped, and to show us a path that is *safer than the known way*.

We are moving from empirical realities to theological ones. We are
hopping continuums that keep us in circular conversations, never going anywhere, at least not anywhere special. I'm done with the sliding
scale spectrum that presents tried, tired, and stale choices. And maybe
you are reading this because you are too. So, let's travel and traverse on
highways and byways dark and untrodden, because if I had to wager, I
imagine it is safer than all that is known; it is *safer than the known way*.

INTRODUCTION

I adore antique and vintage shops. I love things with a story. Things
that have been loved before me. There is a sense of specialness, a storied
nature. Things that don't have a million copies of themselves spread
across the world, just this one that I have found hidden in a back corner
of an over-stuffed, over-junked, second-hand store. I find so much
intrigue and mystery in such pieces. They beg questions that can never
be answered.

I often visit the local antique market every month with my husband.
Every month, one specific seller specifically hunts for old religious
postcards for me to buy. My (atheist) husband, who knows my pen-
chant for old religious art, images, and paraphernalia all too well, plays
a game with me. He looks through all the postcards and tries to suss out
the ones I might like. Once, he handed me several after completing his
usual process. I rifled through the pile, carefully evaluating each one
for a brief moment. I came upon one I was attracted to but also felt
dubious about. It was a classic William Holman Hunt Jesus. Jesus was
holding a lantern and preparing to knock at a door. The image was
filled with light, even though it was nighttime in the picture. Next to

this image of Christ were words from King George VI's 1939 Christmas broadcast speech. He famously quoted Minnie Louise Haskins from her poem "The Gate of the Year," also known as "God Knows." It read,

> I said to the man who stood at the gate of the year:
> "Give me a light that I may tread safely into the unknown."
> And he replied:
> "Go out into the darkness and put your hand into the hand of God.
> That shall be to you better than light and safer than a known way."

At first, I read these words quickly and decided the postcard was worth the 50-pence price tag. As I walked home, I read the lines several times. I couldn't help but see the radical nature of this poem. The sentiments seem to say, forget the Light. Go into the darkness. Because "that shall be to you better than light and safer than the known way."

While King George and Ms. Haskins, I'm sure, had no such authorial intent, my theological imagination took hold. I framed it and placed it on my bookshelf. I dreamed that this was a prayer. A prayer of a Radical Theologian and Post-Christian. A prayer to the Impossible god that leaves the big G God in its dust. Our only hope is the darkness without the Light and all that is better than Light and the *known way*.

Here I am, send me.

Here we are, send us.

Forsaking all we think we know, all that we have worked so desperately to comprehend and dig our heels into, all that we have come to trust, expect and be confident in, we now exchange for the risk of perhaps and a(n) (un)safer (im)possibility.

As I said, I'm just someone who has lived to tell. But that is predicated on the fact that I continue living, wagering and risking every day in ways that I have faith will be *safer than the known way*. In ways that endlessly speak to the human condition, addressing the bottomless desire for wholeness, belonging, and meaning.

What do I mean by all this? Other than getting your mind a bit tongue-tied and speaking ways that sound like a Mad Hatter riddle? To quote John Caputo, suffice it to say, "All that is coming that we cannot see coming."

In chapter one, "A Life after God after a Life after God," I delve into my story. I want to share with you how I arrived at the theological moment of writing this book. It acts as a theological memoir, and covers a lot of ground. I hope that some of you will see your story in mine or maybe some similarities. That there might be some overlapping between our lives and experiences. Nothing happens in a vacuum. The theological wonderings and wanderings in this book certainly didn't. I share my story to be vulnerable with you and recount crucial theological moments in my life in the hope you will allow yourself to be vulnerable.

In chapter two, "Cathedral Ruins," I talk about the hope we have in the destruction. I mark out several events in the 20th century that need to be understood before we can have meaningful conversations about the crisis of Western Christianity. I offer data highlighting the stark decline of Christianity and the church, and why the implosion of our future, with broken promises and broken dreams, is the future of faith's only hope.

In chapter three, "Jesus After Saviorism and Meaning After Metaphysicality," I explore the ways in which Jesus is sold to us from different sides of the supernatural continuum. How both conservative fundamental Evangelicals, as well as liberal mainline Protestants, might be getting it wrong. And if they are getting it wrong, who is getting it right? Is there a right way? How do we engage and respond to Jesus after we have moved on from personal savior motifs and other incomplete interpretations of Jesus, scripture, and god?

In chapter four, "The Reprise of the Madman and Radical Theology," I revisit Friedrich Nietzsche, his madman that runs into the town square announcing the death of God, and all that phrase leads to. I talk about Radical Theology and what it might offer a post-Christian conversation that needs meaningful faith engagement.

In chapter five, "Deconstruction Then, Now and as It May Be to Come, Perhaps," I take a deep dive into a buzzword as of late, deconstruction. Where did it originate? What does it really mean? And the bewitching, wicked, and vexing big, little, limitless concept of "perhaps" and the work of Jacques Derrida.

In chapter six, "A Theological Imagination for the Future," I present helpful theological frameworks as we attempt to have new conversations about god, faith, meaning, and what it means to be human in light of it all.

In chapter seven, "Why the Christian in Post-Christian," I break down the post in post-Christian and the Christian in post-Christian. What does it mean to be post anything, and why Christian? Is there still a meaningful and unique Christian distinctive for us to identify with?

In chapter eight, "He is not here...," I imagine where we might look for god, if we are to look for god. And why where we might expect to look is the last place we should. I look to the resurrection to teach us a thing or two and delve further into what the kingdom of god might be.

In chapter nine, "Our Little Mess and Dust Everywhere," I ask you to go past the edge of the map, recognizing how little we know, but resting in a hope beyond hope and a faith beyond faith of a very worthy pursuit.

In short, this book is the book I wish I had when I grew more curious about my faith, and tried to follow those curiosities. Being brave in the face of fear, I pressed through the grief, pain, loss, and loneliness. This book is the blood, sweat, and tears of my years of risk-taking, saying yes, saying no, and, of course, saying *perhaps*. I have combined years of scholarship and research to offer you language, thought, courage and a dispensation of peace for your journey ahead. I have compiled years of my own journey, study, teaching, travel, and a bit of foolish wisdom. Perhaps it will make sense to you, but with any luck, it will sound more like you've fallen down the rabbit hole, and that will be a sign you are reading it right.

Happy reading, my friend. I have written this for a younger me and a present and future you.

"I was wondering what it would be like to fly."
"Why would you spend your time thinking about such an impossible thing?"

— **Alice and Hamish, Alice in Wonderland**

1

A LIFE AFTER GOD
AFTER A LIFE AFTER
GOD

"There is a possibility for a theology after the Death of God theology because we can be released from the past. We are not done with the word 'god' yet."[1]

— Jeffrey Robbins

I FIRST HEARD THESE words in May 2017. Robbins was speaking at the Wake Festival in Belfast, having published his book, *Radical Theology: A Vision for Change*, a few months prior. Hearing his words woke theological ghosts that had haunted me for years. But Robbins' words also gave me a sense of comfort; belonging. It's as if he'd given my roaming and roving theological thoughts a home. It's a funny thing to speak of home. One can only do so if one knows where home is.

This has always been a moving target for me. I left the house I grew up in on Long Island in New York at 18 years old to go to college in the Midwest and I never moved back. While I visit often, I have had many homes since New York. Home is always temporary for me. I didn't always know it, but my life has been about moments and movements. These fleeting moments would live until the wind changed and moved me on again. I have accepted this, invited it in, and now pay sacred heed to the churnings and yearnings of such moments. Whether I sense change afoot or feel a compelling need to stay, I listen. These instances of transition have become decision-making partners in my life.

While others have referred to me as nomadic, that term feels disconnected from a journey and a story. To be nomadic suggests that, after one has had their fill, they move on, randomly selecting places to rest their head. This has not been my life, although I know very well when to move on. Haphazard maybe to the naked eye, but elegant, with flashes of alchemy and a disruptive peace, urging me into what seems like darkness, yet I know that it is and will be *safer than the known way*.

I've written this book for Christians who feel lost and theologically homeless. Like me, your ideas of Christianity have evolved beyond the confines of traditional notions of God, faith, and belief (the known way). But now, you have more questions than answers. Most importantly, is there still a place for Christianity without a certain construct of God, worship, and rhetoric? The simple answer is yes. The challenge is how. To help you navigate to a path that's *safer than the known way*, let me guide you through my faith journey and how I came to my lightbulb moment in a dingy pub in Belfast.

URIOUSER

e cat, but that's because one's questions
elcome if they disrupted the status quo. But,
been for a long time. It would be years before I
would use terms like *unsettled* and *haunted* to try and convey all that
was inseparable from my curiosity and all that informed it.

The kids nowadays call this curiosity "deconstruction." Back in the
'90s, curiosity meant you were in danger of backsliding, where your
story is cut–severed. Backsliders were those who experienced a harsh
departure from their traditional spiritual trajectory and walked away
from it all. Was it all for nothing? Our identities torn to shreds and
an inability to pick up the pieces. Nowhere to go with it all? For me,
curiosity has always been a consistent thread running through my faith
story.

My oldest recollection of my curiosity was when I was a little girl
walking into my local Catholic Parish on Long Island, New York. I
have a very distinct memory of that church. I could hear the sounds
of the heels of my shoes tapping on the floor as I crept in. I remember
the clanking of the door as it shut behind me, the echo of the hymnals
touching down on the pews, and the faint coughing coming from a
distant corner. There was the white noise of whispering from gathered
pilgrims praying, bent down upon the padded kneelers. This church,
which is a normal size, felt enormous.

Every time I walked in, I looked up. The ceiling, with its crossed
beams, seemed so high. In the front of the church, at the top of the
altar, stood a large wooden cross with Jesus' effigy. It seemed untouch-

able, and I wanted to be quiet in the presence of wha[...]
It felt big and great. It felt strong and filled me with a[...]
but also curiosity. I sensed I was in the presence of the unexpl[...]
something bigger than me–bigger than all of us. Deep in the cor[...]
my bones, I felt the urge to seek out the mystery. These questions I so[...]
earnestly had as a young Italian-Catholic girl, despite making all the
sacraments, going to religion classes, going to confession to shoot the
breeze with the Priest, and lighting all the candles I had quarters for,
were seemingly answered when I 'found Jesus' as a young Evangelical.
The holiness, the awe, the fear, the reverence, the love, it all had a name.
And it was Jesus. At a Wednesday night youth group worship service,
I raised my hand as my emotions surged and gave my life to Christ. I
was 12. I knew no one. I sat in the front row, paid attention, focused
on the preacher, and took it all in. As I raised my hand, I started to sob.
Like a belly cry. Sobbing, hiccuping, almost hyperventilating, as tears
flooded my eyes. The flood of emotion was unstoppable. Some youth
workers (as they were called) came and laid hands on me, which felt
completely normal at the time and prayed for me.

I didn't know what I was experiencing. But if I had to guess, it was
the unpromisable promise that I was loved, cared for, and would never
be alone. In the midst of an unstable childhood and adolescence, I put
my hand up to someone promising me that they would never leave me
or forsake me. They were promising to fix anything wrong with me and
make me better. That they would remove me from any danger, and I
never had to worry about anything ever again.

Except I did worry because I had new and disquieting investigations
start to surface, more curiosities that simply would not allow query.

I remember returning from a youth group retreat on a bus. I was at the front talking with some youth workers. There was something deeply troubling to me that I couldn't wrap my head around. No matter how much I pushed it down, prayed about it, or tried to have confidence in my decision to 'get saved' I couldn't shake the matter of the 'Lamb's Book of Life.' This was the linchpin of salvation messages and altar calls for Evangelical kids everywhere. Such a scary little proposition, especially for children. Apparently, there was a book–a big book. And it belonged to the 'Lamb of God,'—Jesus. It contained the names of everyone who would go to heaven. If you wanted your name in the book, then raise your hand, go forward, and pray with someone at the front. Of course, children and youth do this because the alternative is hell, and no kid wants that.

I asked one of the youth workers about this book. I asked, "what if my name isn't written in there? What if I am saved now, but in years to come, I change my mind or fall away or backslide? What if I am doing it wrong even now? What if I think my name is written, but it actually isn't, or it could be, but it won't because God knows it will change and I'm guessing he doesn't actually erase names, he probably just never adds them in the first place?"

I remember their blank faces. They just stared at me and had no idea what to say. I'm not sure they had ever thought of these questions. I must have been 12 or 13. They were 18-25 and grew up in the same religious process I had just started. I could see how there would be gaps in their theological understanding and biblical knowledge, to say the least. I was met with incredulousness and ignorance. Their fumbled response was that I shouldn't worry about it. Not about this, not about anything. God was in control, as I heard Twila Paris sing on the

Christian radio station. Twila sang it. These guys are saying it. So I guess I'm going to believe it.

I wasn't to worry. I would not fret, or wonder, or wander, and I certainly didn't interrogate, examine, or probe. I wasn't supposed to expose my faith to imagination. It was not given to nuance, complexity, dimensionality, or the like. In other words, it was not human. Transcendent? Yes. Otherworldly, supernatural, metaphysical? Yes, yes, yes. But not human. I didn't think too much. I just knew. And I *just knew* I didn't have to worry.

So, there I was, not worrying about anything. Heaven? Check! Jesus in my heart? Check! Sexual purity/virginity intact? Check! Reading my bible to see what God has for me each day? Check! My story never came into it. Why? Because I was told I was broken and my story was broken, and God would give me a new one. And this story was that I was a sinner, and God had his only son die to take my sins on a cross, so I no longer had to carry them. Done. "It is finished." That was the extent of that story. But even then, I had questions. "If God is more powerful than Satan, then why did God have to appease Satan? Surely, they aren't equal? There is no way they would have to transact tit for tat. Why couldn't God just decree it so and snap his fingers and *then* have it be 'finished?' And if Jesus truly had to die to seal the deal, then why on a cross? Why with nails? Why a crown of thorns?" I had so many questions (as usual).

No one could, tried, or ever wanted to answer these questions. I wasn't even given so much as the context of the cross. No one ever told me about Rome, Caesar, or empire. Certainly, not Second Temple Judaism. Nothing of the historical, religious, and cultural moment first-century Palestinian Jews found themselves in. No real understanding of why Jesus might have been so important and so dangerous.

The God with all the answers, or as Radical Theologian John Caputo calls it, "a ready-with-an-answer religion,"[2] was silent this time. And so were its people.

In my "not worrying" Christianity, living as a "humble" servant of Jesus, I became arrogant. But who wouldn't be arrogant with the Son of God as their best friend, their boyfriend, and their savior? My questions went away, and I learned not to have any more for a very long time.

THE SEED OF STORY, THE SEED OF CHANGE

I was in my senior year at bible college in Minneapolis, MN, in the Fall of 2004. I was a Pastoral Studies major and had taken all the required preaching courses. I could preach a mean three-point sermon, that would leave you feeling convicted when I was done. I could see there was a bonus homiletics class (the art of preaching and writing sermons) offered as an elective. It was called *Narrative Preaching*. I was intrigued, so I signed up.

For the first time in my life, I was recognizing that perhaps I was a part of a story—and interacting with scripture wasn't simply a transaction or an economy of exchange. There was narrative continuity and context to these micro-stories about Jesus. It was powerful, exciting, and transformative. My curiosity was piqued, and I wanted to know more. I just wanted more story, more of *the* story.

A few years later, I started my attempt at seminary. I sat in those early hermeneutics classes and learned that you couldn't just open the Bible and point to a verse and interpret it purely for yourself. But that, while the Bible was beautiful and sacred, it was also literature and should be treated as such. How do we interpret and understand anything we read, hear, or engage? We do so on the basis of the larger story in which it's nestled. We put the pieces of the puzzle together based on all we know of the story up until that moment, and we see it all as a communicative force that has intent. Where is it going? What is its intention? How is it inviting us in? What is our response?

This was and is the beauty of hermeneutics, interpretation, story, and treating the text respectfully. For the first time, I started to grasp that the Bible wasn't the Jesus and me story, but it was the Jesus and humanity story, and I was beautifully and simply a part of it. This is a living story—and we are all invited. Not only that, we're just a small part of the plot. There was and is a bigger story happening here. I heard the term "metanarrative" for the first time, and I was lost to it. I knew there was so much more out there. I didn't know what it all was or what it held, but I was going to find out.

Tom Wright was a scholar who often featured in my early seminary education. His theological views are "safe" compared to my current thoughts. But, in my early 20s, his work was transformative. I read so much of his published work. At the time, he had released a new book called, *Simply Christian: Why Christianity Makes Sense.* Wright spoke of what he called "the echo of a voice"[3] to describe a "call to justice, this dream of a world (and all of us within it) put to rights."[4]

He describes this echo as a dream that, once you wake up you can barely remember. It was extraordinary and meaningful,[5] but it was a flash. Maybe it was a voice, but more of an echo of a voice. "We want to go back and listen to it again, but having woken up we can't get back into the dream. Other people sometimes tell us it was just a fantasy, and we're half-inclined to believe them...But the voice goes on, calling us, beckoning us, luring us to think there might be such a thing...even though we find it so elusive."[6]

This was exactly it. I could hear the whispers of voices as unintelligible as they were, but as soon as I turned around to see where they were coming from, they were already gone. I couldn't find them, I couldn't search them out. I had to wait until they decided to whisper again. Yet they would vanish as quickly as they came. This romanced me and enchanted me no end. It also took me off the hook for having to have all the answers. There was mystery. There was, indeed, more than we could know or imagine. We really did see through a glass dimly lit. It wasn't loud, and it wasn't obvious. A whisper it certainly was.

I decided to be a fool for the whisper, for the echo. I decided to step into the darkness, following the whispers further. Even though their direction seemed to change every time they dared utter. But pursuing them into the shadows was still, indeed, *safer than the known way.*

It would be a decade before I would come to read the words of John Caputo. It would be years before coming upon the terms he used to speak of whispers and echoes—ghosts, haunting, and *specter.* Caputo used the language of haunting or, as he puts it, "hauntology."[7] He takes off from French philosopher Jacques Derrida's language of "spooked." Caputo says that we are haunted by the ghosts that are to come, the ghosts of the past and the ghosts of the returned.

In caputo's coined "haunto-theology", he says that "we live lives of hope in the hint of the promise of what is to come" and that "we live lives of faith in the unforeseeable, in the coming of what we cannot see coming."[8] He says if we resist the call that the 'spook' inaugurated, then "we fall into despair."[9] There is no going back to life as we knew it, to faith as we knew it, to God as we knew it. Life and reality are irrevocably changed, and there is nothing we can do about it. To turn back would be unthinkable and unbearable despair, and to suppress all that we have been prompted and provoked by. But to go forward very (im)possibly means a fall down the rabbit hole. It is an adventure, dark, strenuous, and mind-bending. It introduces to us a new way of being, which is a life of uncertainty and unknowing, and it liberates us from constructs that we didn't know were constructs until...we did.

I was ready for Caputo's words of spectral disruption. I was ready for Derrida's haunting and taunting ghostly encounters. I had been prepared for it, although I had not planned for it. I took the risk and followed the phantoms because I knew I wasn't done with the word god yet. This is post-Christianity and this is traveling *safer than the known way*.

ON BRAVERY, FEAR, TRAIN RIDES, AND DREAMY FRENCH VILLAGES

A lot of my early adult life had been spent living in Minneapolis/St. Paul. I moved there as a student at 18. By the time I was 24, I was married, in seminary, and a full resident. At 31, I found myself divorced, not in seminary, and ready for change.

I somehow went from Italian New York Catholic girl, turned Charismatic Evangelical, youth group, missions trips, purity rings, and Jesus living in my heart, to full-on Pentecostal Assembly of God, to Progressive Evangelical, to post-Evangelical, to...this. Only I didn't know what *this* was. In my 20s, I found myself deeply unhappy with and in my marriage. I was also unsatisfied with my academic pursuits, unfulfilled in my job, and diligently volunteering for ministry opportunities hoping someday I would be offered that paid position and put my pastoral studies major from Bible College to good use. It was all hard to face.

My Christianity was a way of keeping my cool, or so I thought. It was a way of hoping for a better day when it would all work. Because when we didn't like the things we could see, we could lay our hope in all that was unseen. It would all work out. *I'm fine. You're fine. It's all fine.* Until it wasn't. Until I was so unhappy, I couldn't see straight. After seven years of being in a marriage that was a result of Evangelical culture and values (and should have never happened in the first place), the only thing that could persuade me to do the unthinkable as a Christian and ask for a divorce was my own health and well being.

I had lived dead for a long time to survive a marriage that wasn't meant for my ex-husband or myself. But one can only live like that for so long before you actually want to be dead rather than actually go on with the farce. You can only force yourself to live a lie for so long until all the muck and toxicity start to overflow. You can't run, you can't hide. You just have to be brave. You don't have to die physically to live dead. You can decide to shut down every last sign of life you possess for good. You can suck it up and ghost your life. These became my two options: Ghost my life or be brave.

I had to have a conversation with myself. I had to be real for the first time in a long time. I had to lower all pretense and hubris. I had to take a long hard look at my life. My broken little life. So much felt lost. I had only dreams, an unclear future, and I was about to eviscerate my past. But I knew if I wanted any chance at a life, I had to be brave. In that moment, I had to do something I had never done before, and for which I had zero imagination.

I'm lucky I had any shred of gumption left. Or maybe it was utter desperation. But I had to get out. And it had to be now. I had to do it not only for myself but for my future self if I wanted there to be a future self (which I very much did). I asked for a divorce and then walked out the door with only my handbag and car keys. I knew I had made a start.

Within a week, I served my ex-husband with divorce papers and then I was off to Chicago for a work trip for a week. One of my former students, when I was an adjunct New Testament professor, knew what a tough time this was for me. I was working full-time in seminary administration. I sunk myself into this work, and I loved it. While my career was getting on quite well, emotionally, I was vapid. I felt limp and lifeless and was simply putting one foot in front of the other. She asked if I wanted her to come with me to Chicago, be a support to me, or to use biblical imagery, an armor bearer. I immediately accepted her offer.

We were on an Amtrak train—Minneapolis to Chicago. I was sipping coffee as I stared out the window at the rapidly moving landscape, trying to gather thoughts and find peace. I watched the speeding scene, and she watched me. She interrupted my gaze by handing me a book. One I had never heard of but would come to realize has been a little literary touchstone for wild women since its publication, *Women Who Run with the Wolves: Myths and Stories of the Wild Woman Archetype*.

I picked it up, and I could have sobbed. I wanted to be a woman who was running with the wolves. I wanted to be wild and free. I wanted to be strong and wise, unstoppable and unquenchable. But I wasn't. I was a shadow of all I thought I might turn out to be. I wasn't even close to being her, but I knew I wanted to be, could be, and would be. From that moment on, I slowly began to focus on becoming the woman of my dreams. This peculiar ambition found its genesis in that moment. She was the goal—emotionally, relationally, mentally, theologically, and philosophically. I didn't know how I would get to her, uncover her, form her, but I knew I was on my way to her.

Prior to my divorce, I found myself post-Evangelical. I had been on a trajectory. My faith was transitioning and moving and becoming. But then everything became broken. How could I consult a God who had also been transitioning with me? Transitioning into silence, vaporizing into the background, as to be free from blame. I wasn't angry, and I wasn't bitter. I didn't cry about it and wasn't thrown for an existential loop. It just was what it was. But what was I? Well, not an atheist, not even an agnostic. I felt like a coaster. I was coasting on what I knew I no longer believed about God, and I wasn't bothered by it. It was lonely, certainly. Not lonely because of the lack of God, but lonely because so many people didn't understand what was happening. To them, I was someone who was "falling away" or "going off the deep end." Or the favorite, old, Evangelical adage and the worst possible destiny for a fundamental Christian, perhaps I had "backslidden." But I was none of those things.

The pipeline usually is progressive Evangelical to liberal mainline Protestantism. I had seen many make the leap and find some semblance of theological contentment, albeit still confinement, within these communities. But it wasn't for me. It didn't resonate. I didn't feel a sense of home (no matter how short), I had no recognition of theological camaraderie, and, to be completely honest, I felt most liberal mainline environments to be bland. I was bored. I was glad to be out of the wrathful judge, penal substitutionary atonement, don't masturbate lest you die and go to eternal fires Evangelical environments. But I certainly wasn't interested in the granola-eating, hippie-like, gardening Jesus that awaited me in more liberal environments full of liberal politics and stale liturgies. It was what the likes of Nick Cave call "a bloodless, placid savior."[10] So, no thanks. To all of it.

I coasted, and I was fine with this. I had waited a long time to coast. To not have to have the answers. To not feel all the epistemological pressure to know. To take a break from being the girl that had a "powerful calling" on her life. So much of Christianity is about knowing. *Blessed Assurance*, isn't that how the hymn goes? Something I was so sure of most of my life had started to crumble like the rest of my life, and while it was painful, I was totally ok with it.

I might have been down but I wasn't out. I was coasting, but open and living with an expectancy for the first time in a long time. And then I met my best friend and colleague, Barry Taylor, in January 2015. Sometimes the start of a friendship, and a chance meeting, can be the start of much else if we let it. When time is split down the middle, demarcated by before and after such an eventful convergence. This was one such meeting. I walked into a room where Barry was, and he was a site to behold. He just has that bit of *je ne c'est quoi* about him. He is magnetic and even electrifying. He carries a mystique that he does not mean to, captivating all the innocent bystanders who simply don't have a chance. There is no way to respond to Barry other than to be in awe of him and adore him. If you don't love him, then you hate him, and that's because you are jealous of him.

e was wearing green camo pants with some sort of French work-
man's jacket and a silk ascot tied close to his neck. He had ginger hair
that was a bit spiked and was wearing small gold hoops with red rubies
accompanied by several silver and leather bracelets and multiple heavy
rings to match. But it was more than just his look. There was an air
about him that was exceptional. You can't not be pulled in, no matter
who you are.

My mother told me of a YouTube clip where Barry was teaching, in
which he said, "God is dead and we are his disciples." He then dropped
the mic and walked off. I laughed when she told me this. I had no idea
what he was talking about, but if Barry said it, then there must be a
good reason.

When I told him about my mother's virtual scavenger hunt, he
laughed and asked me if I knew what that meant. He spoke to me of
Friedrich Nietzsche, the Death of God movement, and about god as
event rather than God as being or object. Talk about a mic drop.

Years into my Evangelical Christianity's slow melt, the big God in the
sky wasn't simply fading into the background, it wasn't merely elusive,
but it was gone. Expired. It's time was up. In that moment, I realized
that God was, indeed, dead. And I wasn't an atheist or agnostic, I was
a disciple of this dead God, like Barry spoke of in his lecture.

When my mother spoke back this phrase that had clearly alarmed
her, I found myself also shocked. But, more importantly, I was curious.

By the Spring of 2016, I found myself on my way to the South of
France, accepting an opportunity to live and work in a small village for
six months (which turned into a year and a half). Taking this opportunity was another moment of movement when the wind changed, and
I knew it was time to move on and take a chance on change.

When I arrived in Nice, I quickly became acquainted with the surroundings of my new life in France and the work ahead of me. I traveled 25 minutes up into the foothills of the Alpes-Maritimes of the French Riviera, to a beautiful perched village called Saint-Jeannet. For those of you familiar with the famous Alfred Hitchcock film, *To Catch a Thief*, starring Grace Kelly and Carry Grant, Saint-Jeannet can be seen in one of the opening scenes as Carry Grant makes his screen debut. A medieval French village. The sort of place French dreams are made of, and I was to live there.

There are things I learned about life, love, and what it looked like to become the woman of my dreams, a woman who could run with the wolves, that I could never have from systematic theology class or from what I thought a relationship with God was. This was life. This was real living. Out in the world. Taking risks. Alone with adventure and always choosing to play your hand in both of those propositions and run. For me, this was *safer than the known way* and a much less traveled path. Which is precisely why it was for me.

After months of travel through France and Italy, having experiences that will live throughout my life, change me, mold me, speak to me the sage wisdom of the ages, make up for lost time, and fulfill dreams that I thought were dead and buried, I had finally found some sense of strength. I started to re-approach things I hadn't touched in years because I felt like such a failure. The weight of shame was too much to carry.

It was a tragic holdover from my Evangelical days that had long since passed. The freedom to share my weaknesses, to ask for help, to say I wasn't ok and I didn't know what to do about it was the fatal casualty. It created utter carnage in my life. When I found something difficult, no matter what it was, I felt zero freedom to ask for help. There was too much worry about what this would say about my relationship with God and how this God did (or apparently did not) look out for me. I was favored, I was a friend of God. I didn't need help. We had it all under control.

This meant I suffered in silence for years until so much of it exploded. Yet somehow, it landed me in a 500-year-old farmhouse in the South of France, with a garden surrounded by fig trees and olive trees, jaunts to Provence, weekend trips to Italy, and a rest from conventional life that even I couldn't have dreamt up.

But I was brave. And I was brave for the future me that would be able to say yes. I wanted to show up for her. And that desire has never once waned.

Among the rest, solace, and strength that started to establish itself in my life, I decided I would go back. Pick up where I left off with theologians and thinkers whose work and research interested me, and study theology that had already started to reticently court me. I had been dipping my toe in Radical Theology and post-theistic thought. As I continued, I proceeded with caution. The last thing I wanted or needed was highfalutin theological prose and propositions telling me what there was to know about God. But I was easing my heart and my mind into different concepts than I was used to. Terms like *event* and *experience*, rather than *being* and *object*. The unknowable, impossible, unnamable god, as opposed to the God we have known, made possible, named, and tamed. Exchanging the big Other in the sky, for the *tout autre*, the wholly other. What did it all mean? I wasn't sure. But I knew it was time to go on a journey once more. Perhaps towards a new 'home.' Maybe a new theological place to rest my head. It wasn't

Christian, it wasn't theistic, it wasn't the God that I had known, what my belief assured me, and what church had taught me. It was post-Christian, post-theist, post-God, post-belief, and post-church. It was all that was next. *really?*

NO MORE CIRCLES AND STALE AIR

I was sitting at a large antique desk in my garden level room of the 500-year-old farmhouse in the South of France where I was living. I had double glass doors with wooden frames, and brass handles leading out into the garden that allowed the light to pour through, with a breeze wafting the curtains in my direction. I picked up one of my top five formative books to date in January 2017, *After God*, by Mark C. Taylor.

I opened Taylor's book and read words that gave language and sentiment to all I had been feeling and forming over the last few years. Words that would go on to define my life and work, "I no longer believe in circles as I once did."[11] It was one of those seminal moments. The coming together of all the shooting stars with no names, the raging fires that ravaged through long-held beliefs and convictions, the stepping out and away from Light into darkness, the eating of apples and expulsions from gardens, the haunting and the taunting of ghosts with tongues I knew not of. Shots fired. With one sentence, I bookended my journey up until that juncture. A new one was about to commence.

> *I no longer believe in circles as I once did.*
> Tears.
> *I no longer believe in circles as I once did.*

Goosebumps.

I no longer believe in circles as I once did.

Looking around because I couldn't believe no one was there to experience this moment with me.

I no longer believe in circles as I once did.

Highlighting, underlining, writing, and marking.

I no longer believe in circles as I once did.

Grabbing for my notebook to capture all I was feeling.

I no longer believe in circles as I once did.

And neither did I.

Circles. Going around and around on the same fixed system. As noble and as steady as that sounds, as safe as it seems to be set, circles are the most dangerous and menacing threat known to faith. Circles turn revelation into religion and communion into confession. We become deceived by the movement that distracts us from the lack of distance clocked.

The circles and schemas we have situated ourselves in are simply past their sell-by dates. They altogether cannot hold or stand up to our humanity that thrives on imagination, regeneration, and reverberation. We need to fall off the edge of the map. We need to refresh and recreate. Our echoes should not return to us as we speak into the void. Yet circles keep us from all of this and more.

Mark Taylor doesn't believe in circles as he once did. And now I didn't either.

After God is the most marked-up book I own and one I have returned to often over the last several years. When I need to feel seen and heard. When I need to know I'm not alone. When I need to be inspired anew for the journey ahead and remember those unequivocal events that irrevocably and most welcomingly changed me forever.

I have written much about this idea of, "no more circles." I have started blogs, I have published under it, I have written and taught lectures all based on this little yet powerful phrase. I even emailed Mark Taylor upon my return to the U.S. with these words as the subject line. To my astonishment, he replied right away and requested we meet a few days later, as I was in New York City.

I somehow made it through those opening lines only to read another powerful thought that would go on further to define part of my work for years to come, "You cannot understand the world today if you do not understand religion. Never has religion been so powerful and so dangerous."[12] And, of course, then the beginning of chapter one, "The 1966 Easter edition of *Time* bore a black cover with the question 'Is God Dead?' emblazoned in large red letters." Throughout this book, it is my intention to explore just how deep this all runs.

Is God Dead? — which God?

A question that is still being asked, addressed, and attempted to be answered. It is a question to be asked individually, collectively, theologically, philosophically, and socially. It is not a question to be asked metaphorically. When we speak of the death of God, we are speaking of the death of our metaphysical, supernatural, cosmological, and transcendental God. The one who has lived on high, ruled in power, and has lived in our hearts. Is this God dead? And if so, what is our response? How does faith fare? Does it fare? Should it? This question will launch a thousand more, some of which we will explore throughout this book.

This brings me back to that little pub in Belfast. After commencing an intense deep dive into the death of God, its genesis, and all it has spurred since, I sat in front of Radical Theologian Jeffrey Robbins hearing him say that half a century after the death of God "we are not done with the word 'god' yet."[13]

I was ready. There was a question presented in his words. A challenge. To what end were we *not done with god* and what does that mean...for everything?

This is what has marked my journey, this is what spirals me forward, off of the circle, persevering and permeating unto a faith unknown, a God dead, and a loyalty to the "Undeconstrucible."[14] While we are post-God, we are not *post-faith* and this is post-Christian.

This is what you are here for. This is why you have decided to read this book. But what does it mean to be post-Christian, and why aren't we done with the word god yet?

2

CATHEDRAL RUINS

"The promise is over. The era of post-future has begun."[1]

— **Franco Berardi**

"No future, no future for you."[2]

— **Sex Pistols**

A WORD ON RUINS

In late August 2017, I was finishing a year and a half abroad and heading back to the states to a doctoral program in which I would study at Cambridge and a job based in Los Angeles working with churches, faith communities and non-profits teaching, coaching and partnering with them to transform the ministries they were doing or about to do. I couldn't wait to start both.

As I was preparing to go back to America after 18 glorious months in the South of France, my friends and I went to Ischia for a two-week holiday. Ischia is a small island off the coast of Napoli, north of Capri. It isn't as glamorous as Capri, and it doesn't garner the same international tourism. But, it's a beautiful, unspoilt part of the world. I loved it. We stayed in a little flat a stone's throw from Aragonese, a tiny island connected to Ischia by a picturesque stone walking bridge. Aragonese is the home of a medieval town complete with a castle, hilltop cafe, torture museum(!), and at the very top, a cathedral. The castle dates back to the 5th century BC, and still stands to this day.

One morning, fuelled by cappuccinos and caprese, we started the massive hike to Aragonese. I knew with every step around corners and through corridors, I was getting closer to something special. I just didn't know how special.

When we arrived at the top, I looked around, and it dawned on me. I was standing in cathedral ruins. I could see the semblance of a stone altar and tiling. There was no roof, pews, or seats. Mostly just rubble with two dates etched into the side of a stone. The original date of construction and the date of its destruction. It read,

Cathedrale:
costruita 1301
distrutta 1809

My friend snapped pictures of me sitting at the frail, fragmented altar. Anything that might have been etched in the stone had been rubbed away by the sure and steady defacing of time. Instead of multi-coloured iridescent light bathing the cathedral floor, daylight poured through 10-foot holes that were once the home of stained glass. The entire ruinous structure was exposed to the open air with a panorama that stole the attention from what remained of this Christian relic. While it's stunning to behold, the cathedral ruins moved me like nothing else. For years, these ruins have been the inspiration for much of my work.

As I sat amongst the ruins in Aragonese, contemplating, my mind drifted to an image I first saw in my early 20s. An old Norman Rockwell image entitled, *Repairing Stained Glass*. It was from the *Saturday Evening Post* cover, April 16th, 1960. The image depicts a man in a church on a tall wooden scaffold repairing a hole in stained glass. I immediately bought a copy and sent it to a few friends. An old mentor of mine responded, "repairing stained glass—noble work." I thought so too. There was something about the image that called to me. Perhaps it was my love for cathedrals and religious imagery? Or a deep sense of knowing that religions desperately needed repair and salvation? I held that image close to my heart, unsure of how it would manifest in my life.

I have long been a fan of cathedrals. From walking into my little Catholic Church as a naive seven-year-old to the 20-something woman who brought a coffee and muffin into the cathedrals of the Twin Cities. I would sit at the back, sip, and think. I've roamed through some of the most famed and grandest cathedrals in Europe. And I'm still clocking miles through the long aisles ornamented with flying buttresses, oil paintings, stained glass, marble, and, of course, ghosts.

There's something about Christian architecture, sacred architecture, that speaks to the interior architecture of my own longing. A longing lying in rubble, like the ruins at Aragonese. But I also have a firm dream and deep conviction that we need rubble and ruin to have any basis for the present and future. Indeed, we build on our traditions and stories, but sometimes that means moving through their ashes.

It was quite a surreal moment sitting at the crumbled altars of Aragonese. After taking a break from so much of my American life, my theological education career, and, more importantly, 'God,' it was clear to me that this was the next step. Sitting in the ruins of it all and seeing all that has crumbled. Naming it and recognizing it. Also, recognizing all that we are longing for. It was important for me to see how my longing had caused me to end up here, in ruins.

I remember thinking to myself, "This is it. This is the dream. Cathedral ruins." Not in the way where I dream of physical churches being destroyed. But in a way where all of us post-Christian pilgrims can sit among the ruins of Western Christianity and dream about what might be next.

It felt good to be at Aragonese and to feel all those things. And while I stopped and appreciated the structures that once were literal manifestations of my longing (and the longing of so many others throughout time and history), now I simply observe the ruins and appreciate the beauty of my past longing. I am grateful for the naming of it and reclaiming of it, and am ready to pursue the new longing for life and my own humanity. I am truly post-God and post-Christian. I don't long for God or Christianity, as it currently stands and is situated in

Western culture. It's why I can look upon the splendor of structure and see it for what it was, and is. It's why I can still engage Christianity as a structure, even though I'm post Christianity. Because I know what it is I am engaging as I do so. The ruins unto all that might be next for our faith pursuit.

No one wants to be jaded and cynical. At least, I don't. But I do want to go forward with eyes wide open, yet finding myself surprised by hope, new life, and all the possibility or, as Radical Theology would say, the *impossibility* of what belief and the impulse of belief might look like now and anew. I don't pray (as it's traditionally defined), but if I did, my prayer for you would be that you are always in awe. Always seeking as much as finding and that you're haunted by the hope of cathedral ruins as you build, rebuild, live and let live.

In Richard Kieckhefer's book, *Theology in Stone*, he opens with a tale of an old English church in which he says, "Here as elsewhere, the old religion lingers."[3] Let's not be a place where the old religion lingers, but, as always, let's be haunted by the past, present, and future that may, if we are lucky, alert and awaken us to all that is coming and is to come.

WHERE ARE WE, AND HOW DID WE GET HERE?

It's no secret that Christianity is in deep decline in America and throughout the West. Over the last several years, I've given many talks and lectures to church leaders and pastors who wonder where it all went wrong and what they can do to salvage the situation. To understand how Christianity arrived here, a place of ruins, dust, and utter impotence, we must reckon with some hard realities, and take note of the historical moments that lead us here. There is a deep sense of *we aren't in Kansas anymore*, but we don't know why or how to articulate it. We can feel it, we can see its effects, but we can't quite explain it.

Perhaps it is because we aren't having the important conversations about the state of affairs of Christianity over the 20th century. Of course, we could talk about the state of Christianity and its trajectory since Constantine baptized the empire in the fourth century, but that is another book entirely. So for all intents and purposes here, I'm limiting this analysis to the 20th century. However, nothing happens in a vacuum and so centuries of thought, power, and progress prop up the following four milestones. We cannot fully examine present-day Christianity and why we may want to be post such a Christianity without paying attention to some of the most important events that lead us here.

Religious landscapes are shifting. New cultural contexts are emerging. New economic realities are forming, and new digital horizons are rising. All this has enacted upon Christianity in the 21st century in ways we cannot ignore, but have clearly tried. There are psychographics to consider—what has Generation X done with God, how have Millennials responded to faith, where are Generation Z's values lying, and what does the Alpha Generation think of it all?

What I have tried to impart to anyone I have taught over the last several years and still continue to, as I speak to mostly Christian audiences, is that to claim Christianity in the 21st century is a matter of responsibility. It is a matter of examining one's mechanism of meaning-making about what transpires when we believe or have belief in something, and what that all looks like embodied in the world. To truly know what it means to claim Christ (or any belief system) is a matter to take seriously. *the content*

These aren't easy conversations. They are scary. They shake our identities, our foundations, and things we thought we knew. The good news is we're having them, and we're having them together.

1966 AND TIME MAGAZINE

One moment that we must be crucially aware of as we have conversations on the future of faith and what it means to be post-Christian, as I mentioned in chapter one, is the 1966 cover of TIME magazine asking the question, "Is God dead?" This is what inaugurated the Death of God theologies that emerged and subsequently Radical Theology, which we will pursue in later chapters. The TIME magazine cover that is now infamous, released poetically on Good Friday, ultimately questioned the premise of the personal God and its place or lack thereof in the life of society.

The article drew upon the work of academics and theologians, Thomas J. Altizer, William Hamilton Paul Van Buren, and Gabriel Vanhanian. Within days, preachers across the U.S. admonished the article from the pulpit, warning congregations of the consequences of a Godless country. TIME, and the theologians whose work was the subject of the article, received an exorbitant amount of hate mail. Religious America was outraged at the audacity and sacrilege in the piece. But John Elson's article wasn't about the domination of New Atheism, it was about the resurgence of the divine where we might least expect it, as opposed to where we absolutely expected it—within the container we have named God.

Sometimes, one's emotive reaction takes over before slow, critical and thoughtful engagement with a subject can occur. It becomes the sole determining factor in the response. There was no time to move slowly and thoughtfully here. TIME's irreverence could not be tolerated in any form. There would be a rise up, a pushback, but under what guise?

THE BIRTH AND RISE TO POWER OF THE RELIGIOUS RIGHT

The Religious Right movement grew its power and affluence in the 1970s. Its agenda? Racism. Its guise? Taking America back in the name of God through family values, law and order, and pro-life rhetoric.

Fundamentalist Evangelicals such as Jerry Falwell, Bob Jones, Paul Weyrich, and Billy Graham, started paying attention to what they were losing: tax exemption. They continued to segregate their schools and institutions even after it was made illegal. Falwell and others saw the denial of tax privileges as a taste of what was to come with 'big government' at the helm. By the late 1970s, Evangelicals began targeting abortion, even though groups, such as Southern Baptists, who boasted some of the most conservative theology, had no problem with abortion. But interest spiked among conservative leaders to distract from their racist policies. Carter was moved out, and Reagan moved in. The rest is history.

THE SECULARIZATION THESIS

When I was a young adolescent Evangelical, I often heard phrases like, *"America was a decade or two out of becoming like Europe."* What they meant was that America was 'turning away from God' and becoming a secular society, much like Europe, which was often demonized by conservative Evangelical Christians. In church, we would often hear cautionary tales of churches becoming museums and the name of God becoming unrecognizable. I remember being both scared and excited. Scared because I believed what they said. I had no reason to distrust the pulpit, the people sitting next to me, or the family and friends who brought me there. We were in this together and had to figure out how to strong-arm God back into America. I was excited because it meant there was work God needed us to do and I was going to be a part of it.

Since my time in France, I have lectured and written on 'God' in Europe as a matter of fascination. I became interested in the regression and shifting of belief in France, and the small pockets of renewal, reinterest, and 'revival.' In fact, in the summer of 2022, I co-authored a chapter[4] on the European reception of John Caputo's work. As an American living abroad, with a personal interest in both the religious stories and trajectories of both North America and Europe, I can tell you that America will never overlap with Europe's philosophical and secular climate. America and Europe have two vastly different narratives and histories. It's unlikely that America will find itself post-God, with a Secular Humanist worldview, any time soon.

However, all that was predicted by the religious was also predicted by the academics only within the academy it was known as *The Sec-*

ularization Thesis. This refers to the belief that as societies progress through modernization and rationalization, religion loses its authority in all aspects of social life and governance. However, as we have seen and will continue to see, the opposite has happened. In fact, in many ways, it seems as if people have never been more interested in religion.

People are disinterested in what they once knew in their memories, in their lives, and as portrayed in history, as religion. Yet people are as curious and as keen as ever to still seek to discover meaning, and therefore turn towards religion, but not religion as business as usual. Rather, where one's faith can be embodied and where one might live out their religious (or non-religious) identities in new ways that make sense for their lives, their communities, and who they are. In ways that no longer buy and trade in the currency of certainty but in ways that lift up uncertainty and subjectivity in the process.

In Harvey Cox's book, *The Future of Faith*, he asserts that while academics predicted the demise of faith and religion, we have observed an unforeseen reinterest. He writes, "Faith is in resurgence, while dogma is dying."[5] More than ever, people are concerned with, curious about, and reimagining what it means to engage religion. With the rise of liberalism the prediction was that people would be less and less interested in the promise of religion and its various ideologies of certainty and brands of belief. However, the opposite has happened.

9/11 AND ITS SURPRISING REPRISAL OF RELIGIOUS INTEREST

One thing that we sometimes seem to forget is that we are living in a post-9/11 era, and we are doing theology and trying to interpret and understand all post-9/11. It's an era characterized by intense, pervasive, and earnest religious activity and a time of moral multi-valence. It's both impossible and irresponsible to simply speak in terms of separation of church and state when so many of the West's decisions are religiously motivated. 9/11 strengthened fundamentalism in every global faith, atheism included.

George W. Bush used the messianic language of Christian scripture to frame America. It was to be a war of good vs. evil, or as most of the world saw it, Christian values vs. Islamic terrorists. The world was tuned in as to how religion would play out and whose 'God' would win. The world had watched planes smash into the Twin Towers in the name of *jihad*. This wasn't just war, it was a crusade. According to George W. Bush, America was the *city on the hill* that would snuff out the darkness.

People felt scared and deeply threatened by Fundamentalist Islam's expansion while viciously rallying behind a commander-in-chief Jesus that would lead us to victory. Patriotism, as so many times before, had become irrevocably enmeshed with what it means to be a follower of Jesus. Christian Nationalism was once again on the rise. And in our current political climate, we find it more dangerous and insidious than ever.

We are living through an unprecedented rate of religious and cultural change. We are no longer connected by a cohesive cultural picture, if we ever were. We live in a world with competing stories about the nature of reality. We need to pay attention to this because it is happening everywhere we look and in all spaces of culture. What many people don't realize is Western culture was built on an understanding of Christianity that's beginning to crumble. The crucial question is why are traditional notions of Christianity collapsing? We must understand the reasons before we can reorient ourselves so that we may find a proclivity and penchantality for a new path that is *safer than the known way*.

We have to ask ourselves, what purpose does religion serve in society? But this isn't so easily answered. In Mark Taylor's book, *About Religion*, he writes,

> Religion is about a certain about. What religion is about, however, remains obscure for it is never quite there—nor is it exactly not there. Religion is about what is always slipping away. It is therefore, impossible to grasp what religion is about—unless, perhaps, what we grasp is the impossibility of grasping. Even when we think we have it surrounded, religion eludes us. This strange slipping away is no mere disappearance but a withdrawal that allows appearances to appear. Though never here what religion is about is not elsewhere.[6]

Again, we find ourselves down the rabbit hole, sitting at the Mad Hatter's tea party, reading Taylor's religious sentiments. It feels like if we turn everything upside down, if we turn everything on its head, then we might find what we are looking for...or not! But it certainly isn't where we think it should be or where we think we should be looking. Everything is changing, and we must pay attention. The landscapes of Christianity have drastically changed in the last half-century. If we don't understand why and how these shifts have occurred, we will continue to feel the tension of a faith that can no longer act and attend to the changing needs of a rapidly changing world, only we won't understand why.

DARK STATS

To understand where Christianity is going, we need to see how and where it is declining. In 2015, there was a landmark study done by Pew Research, in which we were able to see quite evidently and incontestably the decline of Christianity in America. In a published article outlining all the details of the surveys and research, *America's Changing Religious Landscape*,[7] we were able to see what churches, pastors, and offering plates had been feeling for years. Between 2007 and 2014, five million fewer Americans identified as Christian. However, the number of religiously unaffiliated Americans was on the rise by 19 million within the same period. These unaffiliated Americans, now referred to as the "nones" (coined by Pew Research in their 2012 article *"Nones" on the Rise*[8]), totalled 56 million, second only to Protestant Evangelicals.

Out of the demographic known as "nones" 31% identified as Atheists or Agnostics, 39% identified as nothing in particular, and 30% said that religion is important, but that number is dropping steadily. In the same study, less than 60% of Millennials identified with Christianity. Well, I am a Millennial. Maybe an elder Millennial, but a Millennial still. I remember being in my 20s and everyone in my Evangelical circles was talking about how to 'reach' the Millennials. But now, in those same circles, there is a new concern for Generation Z.

According to a study put out by the Barna Group and Impact 360 Institute,[9] only 4% of Generation Z, comprising 69 million teens and children, claim to hold a biblical worldview. It's clear that there is little interest in what the Bible might be saying, illuminating, prescribing, or communicating. All the evidence suggests that Generation Z is post-Christian, and it's easy to see why. In fact, the Barna report goes as far as to say that "Gen Z clashes with Christianity."[10] Everything they value is often the opposite of everything posited by 20th-century Christianity.

Within Pew Research's study, they took care to note not everyone is leaving. So who is staying, and what is happening with them? While Catholics, Protestant Mainline, and Evangelicals are declining in numbers, they are growing more diverse. This means their arc is changing and their landscape is slowly being impacted by new narratives driven by differing ethnicities, economic status, education, etc. Another important finding was the aging populations of these Christian affiliations. The median age is getting older. So, a congregation with a median age of 40 will have a median age of 50 in ten years, which points to a continually aging population.

This is the most cited study demonstrating Christianity's decline in America. However, several years on from this research, where are we now, and what of the rest of the West and their relationship to Christianity?

In September 2022, a new Pew Research study was published entitled, *Modeling the Future of Religion in America*, and it indicates this isn't just an American issue. "In Great Britain, for example, "nones" surpassed Christians to become the largest group in 2009...in the Netherlands, disaffiliation accelerated in the 1970s, and 47% of adults now say they are Christians."[11]

The interesting piece is that those who are religiously unaffiliated aren't completely "non-believing." Studies show that "many religious "nones" partake in traditional religious practices despite their lack of religious identity, including a solid majority who believe in some kind of higher power or spiritual force."[12] Irrespective of this fact, studies still indicate that it is entirely possible that by 2070 less than half of Americans will identify as Christian, and the "nones" would be as high as 41%.

From the work I've done in the last several years and the countless conversations I've had, it's clear Christianity's decline is about a mindset. It is a steady change of values and ethos, and it is no respecter of age. Across generations, the questions moving people away from traditional notions of Christianity and monotheistic understandings of god are the same. Christianity as we know it cannot persist. When we draw from important research centered in demographics, we can get a good idea of where the institution of Christianity is heading, as those who seem to officially change their religious identities toward "none" typically happens between 15 and 29. Yet we are seeing now more than ever adults between 30 and 65 making an impact on this trend.

It hasn't let up. "People [are] voluntarily leaving religion behind."[13] They can see the ruins a mile away. They aren't jumping ship because they don't have loyalty to the captain. They are jumping ship because they have loyalty to themselves. They can no longer force themselves to live in the tension that the big Other in the sky, the interventionist and personal, moral God, poses to their own sense of reason, intellect, thoughtfulness and post-modern sensibilities. They have to get out. But get out unto what? The move towards atheism and agnosticism often happens because there is a lack of any other options—the choice of this circle or that one. All going around and around on the great wheel of binaries, modernity, and total lack of imagination for anything beyond it, anything that might be next.

They stand, like me and like you, in cathedral ruins, wondering if there is little more to be done than stand among the dust of our hopes and dreams until we become dust ourselves.

NO FUTURE AND ITS INADVERTENT INVITATION

Some years ago, I gave a lecture at an event called Leadership Academy in Indianapolis. I was speaking to a group of church planters for a liberal mainline Christian denomination. They wanted me to teach about the theological climate they find themselves in as they move forward with their vision and dream of starting a new faith community. I find it is getting increasingly difficult to speak to this particular vocation, as it seems we are living in one of the hardest moments to be planting a church in Western society. I decided to be honest and tell them the future is bleak and has failed us. But the future's failure provides the perfect position of advantage for re-creation, re-imagination, and re-configuration.

Italian media activist Franco Berardi's book, *After the Future*, opens with these words, "What happens to political thought, practice, and imagination when it loses hold on 'the future'? It goes into crisis."[14] A poignant opening line from his preface writers. This is precisely where we find ourselves. Set before a future in relentless crisis. Not unlike our gods, our religions, our ghosts, and ourselves. Everything is intensely vulnerable due to its precarious and problematic foundation. Of course, we now find our future, as well as our present, in ruins, as none of the promises of the past were kept. These promises have failed us and our future.

Berardi has been a major player in the Italian worker movements that started in the late 1970s and is a formidable voice in the conversation on digital capitalism, which essentially cellularizes and compartmentalizes the work of the worker. He explains that humanity wasn't meant for, nor can it take, this kind of fragmentation, not our "cognitive, communicative or our emotional capacities."[15] The robust and sexy, yet empty, promise of capitalism, now turned digital capitalism, has killed the future. Berardi tells us that the future is over. As young Greta Thunberg said in her potent and contemptuous speech to the UN during the Climate Change Summit in 2019, "Fairytales of eternal economic growth."[16] The collapse of the future has depressed society, a sick society, according to Berardi. He says that "the progressive commercialization of culture, deadening of metropolitan life, loss of solidarity and insidious dispersal of mechanisms of competition" has positioned us for and towards "existential precarity."[17]

We live in this crazy time of "infinite and invasive" power and capital and a time of narcissistic response to the common good of community. Berardi says, "Depression is born out of the dispersion of the community's immediacy."[18] In other words, depression occurs when the community loses its cohesiveness, power, and traction. The slow erosion of hope and possibility leads to abasement and despair. This happens when communities are fragmented and disempowered. Depression emerges. So, how has this devastated the future? Because "autonomous and desiring politics was a proliferating community." When the proliferating power is lost, the social becomes a place of depression."[19]

The 20th century was a century that promised the future and that trust was not honored. Much like the Sex Pistols' punk announcement, "No future, no future for you!" Even with all the movements, collectives, activism, and grassroots campaigns, "the lack of public sphere [and] the void of collective imagination"[20] is glaring, dismal and, some like Berardi say, impossible.

So, it seems the future has failed us, and perhaps the only hope we have in navigating towards a viable future is the reconstitution of community. To integrate what has been critically and almost fatally fragmented. Community has always been the hope of the future and it has always lived vibrantly in the Judeo-Christian imagination. As we recall a most famous and transformative story reconstituting community, we see a reinstatement of a collective that had been divided and diverted due to the empty promises of wealth, power, and profit. We find in Genesis 11:1-11 the story of the Tower of Babel. A community disintegrated in their drive for power, knowledge, wealth, and prestige. In Acts 2:1-13 we see a reprise of Babel, with their community restored through the speaking of each other's languages, taking part in Jesus' new creation and new community. In another example, we see in 2 Kings 17:6, the loss of ten out of the twelve tribes. And in Mark 3 (and other places in the gospels), we find Jesus calling twelve disciples as a symbol for a reconstituted Israel that had nothing to do with bloodline. All things were being made new; all things can be made new again and again. That is the call, the mission, and the charge.

This doesn't change as we find ourselves post-Christian. In fact, it intensifies as we behold the ruins we find ourselves in. This is what a disintegrated future that has been blown to bits offers us; a chance to take part in the continuing work of faith and engage the possibilities of the impossible! Making all things new, including new promises and new chances to make good on those promises. Promises based within the horizons of reconfigured and transfigured imaginations for a future that draws community together in more meaningful, substantial, healing, and transformative ways. And we can only do this because the expected is blown away. Now we get to decide what is next and best for the future.

CRYING IN THE CHAPEL

Anyone who knows me well, no matter how unexpected, knows I have been an Elvis Presley fan since I was born. I owe this to my dad, who used to dance with me to early Elvis rock 'n' roll that we played on our double cassette player at home in the late 80s. He would swing me up in the air in full 1950s style. I remember having so much fun. I watched all the Elvis movies, listened to all the songs, and collected all the memorabilia I could. Of course, I grew out of my Elvis phase, but every once in a while, when the mood strikes, I'll have a little nostalgic listen.

This past summer, I went to see the new Baz Luhrmann film, "Elvis." When I sat down in the theater, as the opening scene started to play with a far-off sounding *Suspicious Minds*, I started to tear up. When the film was over, I just sat there and sobbed. Elvis' is a sad story on many levels. And amid so much tragedy in the world, all you need is the portrayal of one tragedy to just sit and cry over all of it. Which is exactly what I did.

I was haunted by this film for weeks. I watched interviews with Austin Butler, who portrayed Elvis so bewitchingly, and listened to the remixes on the soundtrack endlessly and returned to Elvis' singing of hymns befittingly. In all my years of Elvis fandom, I hadn't done one thing: listen to the renditions of his beloved hymns and gospel singing. I'm no fan of hymns. I've always found them old, stuffy, and the production of another time, even at the height of my Evangelicalism. Also, Elvis singing hymns, to me, was quite rich! He seemed a bit of a fraud. But after seeing how much he loved gospel music and the effect it had on his musical creativity, I decided to listen. So, I went to one of my favorite coffee shops, ordered a latte, sat outside with my sunglasses on and my AirPods in, and tried to hear his feeling in those hymns. His song *Crying in the Chapel* was brought to mind, so I started with that. It was a revelation (if I could use such religious language).

Isn't this what we are all doing? Crying in the chapel? Most of you reading this book have had a long and arduous journey with Christianity, and you are now identifying as an outsider, an outlier, post-Christian and post-God. But there is a reason we are post-theist and not a-theist. It is because Christianity will always be a part of our story. We can't change that and don't necessarily want to. We will always live after our Christianity, after our God stories that have made us who we are. So even though the chapels of our spiritualities are dead in some sense, aren't we still living in the ruins of them? Aren't we sitting in the aftermath crying? It feels like our lives are one big sob. A sense of groaning and growing. This comes with pangs. This comes with an outstretching of thoughts and movements that would have been impossible had we not been post all that we were before, yet living in light of it.

We are ever transforming forward. This all feels like a perpetual cry. Not out of sadness, but as a release. An ongoing release and letting go unto what is next, while standing on our precious stories that are filled with grace, gratitude, gumption, and, of course, ghosts. And therefore, we cry in the chapel. For the goodness, for the sadness, for all that we have been and all that we will be. For our Gods that have died, for our gods that live, for all that has been done wrong to us, for the wrong we have done to others. For the humble beauty that comes to us still, for all that we are doing and have still left to do. We cry in our chapels, alone and together. And this is a beautiful thing.

It's ok to cry in the chapel, both figuratively and literally. It's ok to sit in that cathedral or stand in that church and cry. For all the ways it has let you and the world down. It's ok to cry because you still find hope. It's ok to cry because you still see beauty. And it's ok to cry because you feel nothing where you once felt so many somethings. Because you aren't alone. We cry and sob and weep and wail together through life. Our human condition is too beautiful and full of ache not to.

So I cry for Elvis. Sure. I cry for myself. I cry for what I lost. I cry for all I have been given and gifted. I cry for my dead God(s). I cry for the empowerment of living confidently in the things we can have confidence in—love and uncertainty. But the whole time, I find I am crying in the chapel, where I will always cry. In the misshapen, chaotic interior of my once-lived spirituality, filled with the holiness and hollowness of tragedy, spiraling forward in the blessed assurance that all that holds me is all I want to be held by.

Somehow we are still here. All of us. If anyone is still interested in Christianity, even those who are post-Christianity, in the West and in the U.S., it is because, as Graham Ward writes in *Theology and Religion: Why it Matters*, they want "to understand something about the world they are living in."[21] What does our faith say about the world we live in and, more importantly, the world we want to live in? What does it communicate about the future we want to build? What makes our faith distinctive, intelligible, and able to be articulated while at the same time versed in the resolve of the unknowable?

When we can't answer the question of what it means to be Christian outside of regurgitated doctrine passed down to us from a pulpit that can't really stand up in the lives we live, that is when the data of decline really comes to life. Engaging post-Christian faith, post-theist thought, and, as we will explore, various understandings of Radical Theology will not only deliver us faith that is encountered by the fullness of our humanity. It will render impotent the need to believe in mechanisms of certainty and instead move us towards a faith that is malleable, adaptable, centered in our social locations and contexts, and provide a way into the world instead of a way out of it.

We do not have to check our theological and spiritual narratives at the door simply because we don't fit into some category that wasn't meant for us and our journeys. Just because we cannot accommodate a model of Christianity from yesteryear that is being relentlessly yet tiredly dragged into the future doesn't mean we don't get to continue in our faith journeys as we work it all out with fear and trembling.

In Gianni Vattimo's *After Christianity,* he starts out by referencing a moment on a public telephone with a former professor of his who was a staunch believer. He was asked the question of whether he still believed in god. Vattimo's answer? "Well, I believe that I believe." [22] What does he mean by this? There are two seemingly opposing translations of the Italian word meaning to believe. Firstly, to believe means "having faith, conviction or certainty in something." However, the other means to "opine-that is to think with a certain degree of uncertainty." [23] Therefore, Vattimo believes with certainty that he believes, uncertainly. He has absolute faith in the lack of absolute. Faith is a risky wager. We believe that we believe. We have faith in the uncertainty of our faith. Ultimately, having faith means that we engage with conviction and uncertainty. *as-if,*

In all this, we must ask ourselves what we want to recover and for what purpose? What do we want our future to look like, and how do we want to reinvest our energies in search of the sacred? I use the term sacred loosely. Because we are not in search of the god in the sky. We are now oriented back in the direction of the world, in the glorious plurality of history and the non-singular nature of reality.

3

JESUS AFTER SAVIORISM AND MEANING AFTER METAPHYSICALITY

"When I speak of the "insistence of God" I mean that God does not exist or subsist but that God insists, while it is the world that exists. God's insistence requires God's inexistence. The world's existence requires God's insistence. The name of God is the name of an insistent call or solicitation that is listed upon the world, and whether God comes to exist depends upon whether we resist or assist this insistence."[1]

— John Caputo

ONE OF THE FIRST major pieces we have to reckon with as we move post-Christianity is what to do with Jesus. Every Christian from liberal to conservative, Catholic to Protestant, theist to atheist, thinks they know the answer. Each group who claims to have the answer speaks of a Jesus who reflects their values and ethics. But what purpose does Jesus serve for post-Christians? Does he hold any value beyond the personal savior motif?

Is there Jesus beyond saviorism, and meaning after metaphysicality? In other words, can we have meaningful faith without the promise of the supernatural? And can we have meaning at all without a moral god? These are questions of post-Christianity. Atheism might refer to Jesus as simply a moral teacher or a murdered revolutionary who died an enemy of the state. For traditional Christians, he is the savior of the world, who died for our sins and resurrected from the dead to provide eternal life. But must we pick a side? Is the only option to slide back and forth on such a continuum? Do we have to pick an end of the spectrum?

The danger of these literal and empirical binaries is that we classify faith in terms of whether God exists or not. This means we are still living in the theological stone age, dealing only in matters of truth and non-truths, proven as fact or its fictitious. But there is another way. Not in the postmodern way where truth is a la carte and meaning is for sale. We still find ourselves on a storied trajectory, but as we do so, we understand the implications of that which we are speaking. This is what it means to be post-God, post-theist, and post-Christian. We move on, carrying all we once knew into the future. We build on all the past brought us and all that failed us, or rather simply lived on past its sell-by date.

To engage post-theism, as opposed to atheism or theism, means that we have other interests, better interests. Engaging post-theism, as opposed to atheism or theism, means focusing on the theological over the empirical. When doing this, we render the metaphysical aspects and/or concerns of god irrelevant. The biggest question of faith then becomes not whether god exists but, as John Caputo puts it, how god insists.

This is part of what this book aims to explore, why faith still matters long after the moral god has gone and why theological realities will lead the way. Theological realities don't force us to sign our name on the dotted line when it comes to historicity or facticity. We don't have to buy and sell in currencies of actual and literal. We don't have to talk about a literal resurrection or a literal Adam and Eve, because the theological realities and the transformation it brings give the one-dimensional 'it did or didn't happen' a run for its money.

Our faith gets to be what religion always dreamed it might be. We can rise above categories and boxes. We can move past fundamental silos on both sides(!), both liberal and conservative, and avoid re-entrenchment. All too often, conservative Evangelicals move on to more liberal forms of Christianity. This, of course, is a natural progression for anyone looking for a bigger God. The issue here is that it's the same metaphysical God, but this God is just playing for the other team. There is a new fundamentalism that emerges, and then God in the sky lives evermore, it is just a more palatable and loving one. If one moves on to atheism, particularly the total bore and snooze that is New Atheism, aka Richard Dawkins, et al, then we are still talking of a moral God who has existence, being, and agency. Philosopher Alain de Botton says that, "The most boring and unproductive question one

or apologists

can ask of any religion is whether or not it is true....Attempting to prove the non-existence of God can be entertaining activity for atheists."[2]

Saying 'God's' existence doesn't matter, nullifies the atheist argument. We speak of the promise of god and faith without the white noise of debates regarding existence. Instead, we are invited to see how god might insist and what this means for the future (topics we will explore in later chapters).

Keller - if god insists on existing...

JESUS AFTER SAVIORISM

We have to ask questions of how Christianity continues to impact our lives and culture and how we are going to engage it.

In Jean-Luc Nancy's *Dis-Enclosure: The Deconstruction of Christianity* he writes,

> The de-Christianization of the West is not a hollow phrase but the more that process advances the more it becomes manifest through the fate of immobilized churches and anemic theology. That which still attaches us in many ways to the West is the nervation of Christianity itself. Nietzsche put it very well in saying that the Buddha's shadow remains for a thousand years before the cave in which he died. We are in that shadow, and it is precisely that shadow that we must bring to life. We are in the nervation of Christianity; it holds us, but how?[3]

This is the question we are ultimately trying to answer.

I refer to myself as post-Christian, I'm still within the ...ristianity. I have been called an atheist, a Christian atheist, ...ostic, a backslider, an unbeliever, unorthodox, a heretic and on ...e occasion a wolf in sheep's clothing. I am none of those things. No one gets to dictate my relationship with Christianity.

I'm not looking to topple, debunk, or slander. I am, on the other hand, trying to move through Christianity and faith in a way that becomes meaningful in matters of life and the world. As we are all trying to, together, ask questions of what is next, there are so many doctrinal pieces that we can get hung up on. We know when something no longer makes sense to us, but we don't know where to move next. We feel stuck, theologically, and this causes a myriad of issues.

Jesus is a fascinating figure to say the least. He means a lot of different things to a lot of different people. Jesus is still of great consideration and concern to me. The issue is Jesus is of great concern to a lot of Christians and as a result Jesus becomes completely owned by the ideological values of the group holding him. Whether it is the wrathful judge or the peace-loving pacifist, Jesus is prescribed and described by all who claim to know him. Jesus has been used to justify all diabolical means of power and control. He has been wielded to oppress, to abuse, to colonize. Jesus has been made to hold up racism, homophobia, xenophobia, anti-trans sentiment, antisemitism, Zionism, and Trumpism.

Even liberals have owned Jesus as their poster child for inclusivity, immigration, anti-racism, pro-choice, anti-war sentiments, and the like. Even when the attributes are favorable, it's dangerous territory to claim Jesus as an example to lead the way in the 21st-century. This isn't to say that we can't suspect and infer what Jesus and his world may have honored and appreciated. It just means that we must take great care not to attach Jesus to causes to support our own agendas, no matter how noble they may be. At the end of the day, we are still arguing over the matter of being—a being made in our image.

I have been released from and no longer conform to ideological and doctrinal expectations. I no longer feel pressure to succumb to categories of certainty. This freedom means I don't have the need to only talk about Jesus as a great teacher, an enlightened rabbi, the son of god, or a personal savior. Jesus can be all of those things or none of those things. I don't need to own him, I don't get to own him. If we are genuinely interested in who Jesus was, the text we call scripture, with little sneak peeks and snippets, constructs several pictures for us. This is an ongoing hermeneutical sojourn into narrative, humanity, beauty, and uncertainty. It is nothing we can pin down or domesticate. It *is* something that keeps us on our toes, moves miles when we sometimes move inches, and with each new discovery, we see just how upside down it all is (in the best way!).

As I attempt to speak of Jesus, I do so knowing that language always falls short. I'm also aware that there are infinite ways to speak about Jesus. My goal is to help us move away from the assuredness that keeps our faith rigid and 'safe,' towards an understanding in which our grip is loosened, our hearts are big, our imaginations are wild, and our theologies are generous.

Several years ago, I wrote a piece for a blog I had at the time called "(Im)Personal Jesus." In the article, I spoke about how the priority we give to Jesus being our personal savior is totally superfluous to the mission of Christianity. I talked about how the central figure is not the central point and how if one does indeed have a 'personal relationship' with Jesus then that is a personal choice. More than that it is a private matter and none of anyone else's business. It certainly should not be the litmus test for whether one can be a Christian or not. The whole of the New Testament, and the whole of scripture for that matter, is not about having a personal, one-on-one relationship with Jesus Christ. There are so many other imperatives, so many other calls, implications, narratives, and invitations. Americans in particular have a very short historical memory, and we don't often realize that the rise of individualism within the modern West is deeply linked with the rise of the personal Jesus narrative. With the burgeoning of individualism the communal nature of Christianity is continually undermined.

The article was scandalous, to say the least. Although I didn't write it to be scandalous. I never write for scandal. I wrote it to format my thoughts around this idea. And I believed they were thoughts people needed to hear. You can absolutely engage Christianity, and engage it well, without the 'personal savior living in our hearts' rhetoric. Concerned readers accused me of starting my own religion, blasphemy, and heresy. Readers told stories heralding how real *their* experiences with Jesus were. And my favorite response, simply said, 'what happened to you?' For whatever reason, some people feel threatened and attacked by these ideas. A sure indication of control and fear. With that being said, let me be clear, I am not attacking anyone. I am not even saying that you are 'doing it wrong.' I am simply saying there are other ways to engage faith. I have had to clarify my intentions more than I think is fair. But there you have it.

People of faith find themselves in massive doctrinal crisis because many aspects of Western Christianity have become untenable. One such untenable tenet is the idea of a personal savior; a divine caregiver that lives in our hearts, that we talk to each day, and that we are accountable to in prayer for all of our actions and choices.

So, if the purpose of Jesus isn't savior and if, as stated earlier, Jesus doesn't belong to conservative values *nor* liberal values, then what use is Jesus to us and why does it matter for being post-Christian?

Roger Haight, an American Jesuit Theologian and former President of the Catholic Society of America, wrote a seminal text on Jesus back in 1999. This text resulted in his excommunication and prohibition from teaching in 2004 by Cardinal Joseph Ratzinger (before he became Pope Benedict XVI). In 2009 he was completely silenced by Rome, forbidden to teach or write on all theological matters. With the dawn of Pope Francis, he was somewhat reinstated. This is what happens when you start messing with people's Jesus. And by messing, I simply mean providing other lenses through which to see the man, the myth, and the legend.

Haight, in his book, *Jesus: Symbol of God*, which is absolutely impossible to summarize here, says that "The symbols of a specific culture provide the form of a particular religious consciousness."[4] He goes on to quote Paul Tillich in saying, "Religion is the substance of culture."[5] It's words like these that made him quite misunderstood by his critics, who believed him to be using the secular to appropriate scripture and not the other way around. But that wasn't what he was doing at all. He was simply saying that the gospels weren't written in a vacuum. So, before we make major Christological statements on Jesus and his divinity, can we admit that some serious sociological landscaping is happening in the text that delivers Jesus to us? That is all. And that is where we need to start. Our cultural symbols provide a particular and, oftentimes, shared religious experience. We have to see that, we have to admit that, we have to reckon with it, and then ask, what does this mean for me and for us now and how we might want to interpret Jesus?

He goes on to say that "People encounter God in Jesus, and they still do."[6] Of course they do! Of course *we* do! This doesn't change whether we encounter god in other ways or not at all. Now, of course, as Haight rightly asks, "what does 'to encounter God in Jesus' mean?"[7] This is the question of the critique of the personal savior framework, isn't it? Haight goes on to ask, "Is the medium of this encounter really Jesus or the memory of Jesus?" Thankfully he continues, "But we do not have to solve these problems now."[8] We don't have to answer what seems like unanswerable questions to know that the Jesus movement of the first century, and its impact on Judaism at the end of the second temple period, was phenomenal. We can clearly see that "Jesus is the mediation of God's presence to Christianity."[9] Haight points out that this is the underlying logic as we pursue literary understanding of Jesus being the Christ. And my commentary? Well, perhaps we went the wrong way with our underlying logic.

According to Haight, we may have turned a "historical consciousness into a sectarian confessionalism that will not enter into dialogue with other witnesses to common human experience."[10] This is how I have felt for so long. When you read theologians that articulate so poignantly things you have only clumsily suspected, it feels like another piece of the puzzle falling into place. Although, I would argue, it's a puzzle we won't ever complete.

These are only a few thoughts of how we might start thinking about Jesus as post-Christians. This allows us to explore the notion that, simply, "Jesus makes God present in a saving way."[11] Now this sort of statement packs quite the punch because it opens the door for so much inquiry, study, and, to be honest, freedom. It releases the fettered Jesus from our bonds and projections. We cannot understand Jesus "by projecting actions and behaviors of Jesus outside this world about which in principle we know nothing."[12] Full stop. Outside of this world...about which...we know nothing. Isn't that enough to make us stop and think?

Here's the thing, these statements don't invalidate yours, mine, or anyone else's experiences with Jesus. But, if you have made Christianity exclusively about your personal experiences with Jesus, then you might be missing something.

French philosopher-theologian François Laruelle and his book, *Clandestine Theology* have sent me spinning. I am so encouraged and invigorated by Laruelle's work. In Laruelle's chapter on Jesus entitled, "The Gospels: Models for Non-Christianity," he talks about how the apostle was called in the image of Jesus and not in the image of God. The image of Jesus, as understood through Paul was not only mediated by his Hellenistic understanding of mystical encounters but was also his unique experience. And what was this experience? It was his faith experience. And, unfortunately, sometimes certain brands of faith have "the force to tear a subject from religion."[13] What is the subject here? Well, the clone, aka the apostle, priest, and disciple. And this subject/clone tends to run concurrent to the religion that has been transformed, for better or for worse, by its subject. As this subject or clone is "seduced by the religion-world that he or she will have 'forgotten' to transform it."[14]

Therein lies the rub. Have we been so seduced by religion in terms of its clones in the image of its mediator that we have perhaps forgotten to transform the world? Have we become so wrapped up in the original subject that we have never left it and found ourselves living concurrent to the, perhaps, true purposes of Christianity? These are big questions with massive implications. They are not meant to be answered nor to devastate. Rather to get our minds thinking in new directions. We don't have to have it all figured out. We simply have to allow our theological imagination all the freedom it desperately desires. Perhaps the voices of all those ghosts might come together for a short semblance of a direction past any familiar path, one that leads us down a road *safer than the known way*.

The opening of Laruelle's book reveals to its reader the intention behind the term 'clandestine.' "*Clandestine Theology* sets out the conditions for a systematic distinction between faith and belief. It is clandestine because it does not go through any of the usual paths."[15]

A faith that does not play by the rules and a theological odyssey that is completely off the map are what we are after. At one time in my life, I could be quoted as saying that we need to redraw the map, but I now know we need to escape the map. I once said we need to redraw the grid, but we have to go off the grid.

I have many friends and colleagues who have made similar journeys to me. Every once in a while, they confide in me that they sometimes find themselves missing God. The God that *is a friend that sticks closer than a brother*. The God that welcomes the licentious prodigal back home with a feast. The God your best daydreams could rely on, holding fast in the reverie of believing in the *report of the Lord*. I listen and offer comfort. This is understandable, and the sort of complex trauma the God in the sky and his disciples leave in their wake. However, for me, I don't miss it. It isn't because I am resentful of it or exasperated by it. It is because my faith is doing what it has always done; following the next curious step. Looking up, looking down, looking in, looking out. Searching and searching some more with no expectation of anything being found. Rather it is the search itself, and perhaps the unsearchable nature of the search, that makes it worth searching. It is how we search, and the integrity of that search. It's about not taking the easy way out but rather staying loyal to what Jacques Derrida has termed the *undeconstructible*.

My personal relationship with Jesus has seen its day for a variety of reasons. And the one-on-one nature of my interaction with what I believed to be the God of the universe has been over for some time. People often ask me questions like what triggered its conclusion? Was I sad? Did I grieve? Was I left with a god-shaped void in my life? While I usually give robust responses to questions of faith, these are always hard questions to answer. Mostly because they are simple. The answer is always 'no.' No, I didn't grieve; no, I wasn't sad; no, I don't miss it; and no, there is nothing missing in my life. Nothing is missing, and my life has been incredibly full and wonderful. Certainly not perfect, but certainly extraordinary, because it wasn't a complete departure, it was simply the end of that particular stage of faith. I was post-Jesus as savior. He was no longer living in my heart. I was post the God who had a plan for my life. I was post-savior because *I* was the only one who could save me. I had a plan for my life because I was the only one who could make it happen. All my supernatural friends had met their end.

This is why talking about what comes after Christianity (which is not atheism!) is so important. There is more. There is more faith, there is more life, there is more humanity, there is more freedom, there is more imagination—endlessly so. But we must take the biggest leap of faith to end all leaps of faith. Where does it lead? You guessed it—*safer than the known way.*

THEOLOGICAL REALITIES

Empirical realities are a difficult economy when it comes to meaning and sacrality. Why do we need anything to be strictly empirically or historically true? The absolute truth game is an old, tired circle. Every time you come back around, you are at the same place you started, and none of it made a difference. Why? Because even if finding out the absolute truth about the existence of God and a particular way of locating the divinity of Jesus was possible, we still wouldn't ever be able to 'know' for sure. Which leads me to believe that we can do better than simply defending the existence of God, the facticity of scripture in terms of literal and actual history, and, of course, the theologizing that comes from all of this.

There are theological realities within the text that are so much more moving, powerful, and transformative than simply getting to the bottom of whether or not Mary was a virgin. There are stories that come to us from Paul's letters that eclipse the relevancy of whether or not actual, empirical Paul wrote them. The gospels each tell us a narrative version of the life of Jesus of Nazareth, as each author saw fit with specific theological intent for a given community. It's an utter feat. Yet we are caught up with when they were written, which one came first, and so on and so forth. By doing this, we utterly miss the point and strip these texts of their dignity and magic.

When I first started seminary so many years ago, I remember sitting in one of my first hermeneutics classes and my mouth was constantly dropping to the floor. I was astonished by all I was learning. I remember the first time I started to learn about a literary theory called "Speech Act Theory." Asserted by John L. Austin in his book *How to Do Things with Words*,[16] Speech Act Theory says that all language is communication and performative and that language has three parts—locution, illocution, and perlocution. The locution is the basic sentence—several words strung together. The illocution is the force in which something is being said—what the author wants to communicate. For example, "I'm going to pay you back." Does this mean the author owes you money, are they trying to scare you, is this a threat, or did you do them a favor they would like to return? The locution in and of itself has no inherent meaning. This was Austin's point and entire theory of language. Thirdly, perlocution, which is what the author wants to evoke in their reader/hearer—fear, gratefulness, peace, squaring up the debt? We don't know. We need all three parts of the speech act in order to have any shot at communicative success. Meaning does not lie solely in the words paired together, one after another. Meaning does not lie in authorial intent alone, certainly not empirical authorship, as there is no way of knowing this. Meaning does not lie in the response of the reader alone, certainly not the empirical audience, as we will never be able to access this.

This trifecta is found all within the text. Rather than the empirical or actual author, we want the implied author (the perfect author of the text). Rather than the empirical or actual audience, we want the implied reader/hearer (the perfect reader/hearer located within the text). The text constructs it all for us. We respect and honor the text by remembering this as we read and interpret it.

Why am I telling you this? Because the text is not concerned with empirical stand-alone realities, so why should we? If there is something to be gleaned from the text, then it is up to us as readers and interpreters to do our best to read and engage as the perfect readers; to try and become part of the speech act and watch the world of the text open up as the text builds it for us. When we read the text in ways it was never meant to be read, we handle it inappropriately, birthing dangerous theology in the process.

I remember I was on a train once on my way to meet my good friend for a few days. I was in my early 20s, was new in seminary and was learning so much in all my courses. There was this man sitting next to me on the train. We were stuck together for some hours, so we started chatting. I always cringed having to tell people what I was doing. Once you say you are involved in Christian things, people usually have an automatic idea of what that means. And while I might have been that at one point, I was starting to not be...that. In any case, I was sharing how I was in seminary. He was an atheist and immediately took his best shot at debunking any confidence I might have in the Bible. He went for the Christian jugular: inerrancy and infallibility. Even though I was new at reimagining what those words might mean and how they could possibly be reauthored, reinterpreted, and reimagined, his comments were anti-climatic and didn't phase me. But my lack of reaction must have really phased him.

He proceeded to ask me if I knew about all the inconsistencies and 'errors' in the Bible. He asked me specifically about the gospel of Mark, which I had turned my special attention to at seminary, so he was in luck. He asked me if I knew of the several huge parallels between the gospel of Mark and *The Homeric Epics*. He asked me if I knew that the author of Mark had borrowed plots and literary characters from *The Odyssey* and that they show up in huge ways throughout Mark's gospel.

I cannot tell you the amount of times this sort of thing has been thrown at me in my adult life. It is amazing how many atheists want to throw Christians for loops that they can't recover from. But this is what staking our whole lives in empirical claims of religion can do. It can destroy our identities when poked and prodded. Because if all we have are historical and literal claims, then when they fall, we fall. It has happened so many times, and we are now seeing a mass exodus of American Christianity for these reasons.

I looked my little train neighbor square in the eye and said, 'Yes, I know. It is quite beautiful, actually. That Mark was writing in Greek to Greek people. He would have been very familiar with Homer's stories. Odds are he learned to write by imitating these narratives, and he would have wanted to capture the imagination of his hearers and readers using something with which they could identify. Only 'Mark' makes Jesus even greater than Odysseus, and this is how...'

He had nothing to say. I had taken scripture back from someone who allowed the sun to rise and set on its empirical truth claims, or lack thereof. Christians aren't the only ones holding strong and fast to this classification. Atheists do as well, and they base their entire (a)theology on it.

The author of Mark was human. So were his hearers. He composed his story of Jesus within a social location, and he would have worked hard to make sure his message was clearly understood. He would have been willing to employ whatever was necessary to do so. Including powerful and well-known literary allusions of the time. Why shouldn't this be known and celebrated? Why is this threatening? Why should this sort of information allow what we think of scripture to tumble like a house of cards? Because scripture and all it contains will indeed be a house of cards as long as we value empirical truths over theological ones. Once we remove the empirical, actual, literal piece out of the way, we are free to explore the theological speech acts at work within the text, for better or for worse. We don't have to find justification for all the ugly in the bible, either. Because we can take it on its textual and contextual terms.

Approaching all things theological with a certain hermeneutical humility is desperately needed. A concession right off the bat that we don't know everything, nor do we have the tools to discover everything. Also, transformation is the point, not objectivity. Story, is how we change, how we grow our epistemologies, and how we see more clearly, to know that we don't (and never will) see things fully.

The resurrection is another battleground of empirical and theological realities. Christianity is based on this fundamental moment. But for all those who were like me as a child, who had so many questions. What came before it, after it, around it? Why did there have to be a death? Why did Jesus need to rise from the dead? It all seemed so random. A little bit of theological backstory goes a long way. Now this isn't a commentary, so I'm not going to spend too much time talking about how resurrection was a fairly recent eschatological hope, birthed from the theological imagination of Second Temple Judaism during the exile. God's people needed something to hold onto. A light at the end of the tunnel. They needed to know that this suffering wasn't in vain. In Mark 12, we see the Sadducees didn't believe in the resurrection, as opposed to the Pharisees who did. The Sadducees were the old-school line of priests. An almost aristocratic lineage, likely stemming back to the priests of Solomon's temple. The Pharisees were a relatively new priestly order dating from the Hasmonean Dynasty, just before Roman rule. This is the sort of background that helps to illuminate deeper theological meaning if we let it.

This is a beautiful example and a powerful story of resurrection. That death would come, not only to the individual but what seemed to a people and ethnic group. But no matter what, there was still hope. This hope sustained the diaspora during a period of 400 years of silence from their god, Yahweh. This term resurrection was only to be used in light of the eschatological hope, when God was returning to his people, when everything would be different. This is why Mary, when speaking to Jesus after the death of her brother Lazarus in John 11, concedes that she will see him again, "I know he will rise again in the resurrection at the last day." There was an expectation. This is why it was so powerful and so unbelievable when the news spread of Jesus' resurrection. This is why there were questions as to whether this was Jesus' ghost, apparition, or angel (John 24:37). There was a precedent for these sorts of things. But a 'resurrected' Jesus? This meant it was starting. All they had been waiting on, hoping for, and believing in was about to commence. Not quite in the way they thought it was, but something was about to begin...

This theological reality wakes us up that something is indeed on the move. This is the theological lens that leaves doctrines like penal substitution in its dust! Old, boring, emotionally manipulative and theologically stunted renditions of resurrection tell us that Jesus died for our sins so we could go to heaven. What? In the face of what the text and subtext are telling us about resurrection? Within the hermeneutical horizon of the Speech Act that is taking place? I don't think so. Not interested in that circle. I'm hopping off here.

When we speak of god in light of theological realities and when we talk of Jesus beyond saviorism, we re-lay the groundwork for something entirely different than anything religion and Christianity has told us about god. Even when we choose to go down a path of mysticism, most likely, we are still trying to interact with an objective being of agency, albeit agnostically so. Hopping that track, and changing that trajectory is what being post-Christian is all about. We are now talking past all that we have been sold, forging new and unknown paths *safer than the known way.*

So, it seems that rather than the point being God's existence, perhaps the insistence of god allows for god's existence to be up to us, as John Caputo would claim.[17] "A theology of the event is not supposed to end up in pantheism or reinventing 'panentheism,'...still more meta physics."[18] We are the mediators and interpreters of god's insistence. If god exists, it is because we do. As Caputo urges, "we should be very careful not to attach any metaphysical baggage to such talk or confuse ourselves with God."[19]

We don't need God to exist as being for faith to have a future and for it to be meaningful and transformative. It is a futile and unknowable errand anyway. But still, god does, indeed, insist. Therefore, so does our faith. But how? Let's start to answer this question.

↳ post metaphysics

4

THE REPRISE OF THE MADMAN AND RADICAL THEOLOGY

AHize   final event

"Today, the death of God is really a conversation about the death of the death of God, or living with God in the aftermath of his death. It is about the relationship between the iconic and the idolatrous."[1]

— Barry Taylor

"THE DEATH OF GOD" isn't actually a household phrase, but it almost was in 1966. The truth is many people get the death of God wrong, and I think it's because it sounds aggressive and scary. It also sounds atheistic, irreverent, sacrilegious, and a whole host of other uninviting adjectives.

I can't blame anyone for being alarmed when they hear the words, *god is dead and we are his disciples.* I remember when I was Evangelical, I had a high horse. In other words, if it was scary or something I didn't understand, I hid behind the guise of reverence. If I was asked to do a level of thinking I couldn't square with what I believed, I simply called it irreverent. And I certainly had too much reverence (self-righteousness/ignorance) for my God. My warrior king, Old Testament smiting, Yahweh God turned Jesus, savior of sins and of the world, to listen to anything that might blaspheme or ridicule any of that.

I remember a very well-known Bible teacher at the time, whose work I read and who fanned the flames of my love for Scripture. When *Blue Like Jazz* by Donald Miller came out, she refused to read it because someone told her it was "good but irreverent." She simply wouldn't have it, and she refused to read it. If this excuse was good enough for her, it was good enough for me and good enough for anyone. These days I am much more comfortable with John O'Donohue's idea of reverence, "Ultimately, reverence is respect before mystery."[2] These days I am happy to leave it at that.

It is difficult. I get it. If you allow something to somehow disrupt the foundations of your identity, it is a slippery slope to losing your grip on all you ever thought you knew to be true. Because faith isn't simply a box that we check or a box we can open and close and then shelf again anytime we feel like it. Faith is something that tells us a deep and meaningful story about who we are. It is the bedrock of our identity, and it is how we understand ourselves in the world. And more than that (if it is possible that there is more than that), we trusted something enough to make our lives about it. We took the faith wager. We believed our friends and our families and our churches and our pastors when they spoke of this God and what this God offered. We came to know this God through the experiences of others and how they aided in preparing our own imaginations for what we might expect, what we hoped to expect. And then we communed with this God and believed everything we perceived was being spoken to us, through God's spirit, through God's word, through God's people, through God's creation, all of it. We staked everything on this claim. Salvation, scripture, safety but never sabotage. There was just too much at risk. If we start to engage any curiosity that leads us to any sort of change...well, how does one 'change' the very infrastructure of one's life without it all falling apart. This is truly sabotage, isn't it? This is a crisis of the first order.

So we don't poke around. We specifically don't hunt for ghosts or poking sleeping bears. Why not just let it all lie? Lie, and *lie*.

No. We don't want to ask the question of what is behind a statement like 'god is dead', and no, we don't want to read anything that might introduce something outside of the bounds of our convenient small and constructed truth(s). It is too consequential and severe. After all, didn't *curiosity kill the cat*? We don't want to die, and we don't want our god(s) dead, either.

Hiding behind reverence, hiding behind the cherry-picking of scripture to justify keeping one's mind filled with all that's pure, holy, and good and lovely things, is perhaps because we can't handle what might be beyond. Beyond our curated and informed imaginations. Beyond all the religious rhetoric that keeps the status quo in flow and not in flux. Beyond a level of belief that would have us mortgage our identities. Can we be brave? Can we dare to query and endeavor the adventure? If we can bear the burden of loneliness for a short while, at an attempt to tear the curtain ourselves, we may just get more than we bargained for, if faith was our wager in the first place.

When I encountered my dear friend's words for the first time, *being disciples of a dead God*, it was truly the first time. Throughout bible college and seminary, somehow, I had yet to properly engage Death of God theology, and all that flowed from it. It took me a long time to become conversant with it, to understand the type of death and the type of God it spoke of, and to speak intelligibly about why it matters for our post-Christian lives. I did a lot of reading, a lot of listening, a lot of harkening back and unknowing and unlearning. Because as I explained in the previous chapter, not only can we not understand Christianity in the West today without confronting certain events, but we certainly cannot open ourselves up to all that is unknowable, unnameable, untamable, and uncontainable if we don't understand how the knowable, namable, tameable, and containable has died.

FRIEDRICH NIETZSCHE AND HIS MADMAN

In Friedrich Nietzsche's "Parable of the Madman" from *The Gay Science* in which we see the words, "God is Dead," we find a story of a man running into the town square proclaiming, "God is dead. God remains dead, and we have killed him."[3] According to Carl Raschke, "The saying actually occurs in Hegel's major work *The Phenomenology of Spirit*. Nietzsche merely developed and promulgated such an outlandish proposition with his wild and provocative imagination."[4] In the midst of a god that was nowhere to be found, that was hiding or had disappeared, it was Nietzsche's madman who proclaimed he stood among the "murderers of all murderers."[5] While Nietzsche has been widely misunderstood as a secularist and atheist, in the wake of the Enlightenment, when truth had to be scientifically proven, and faith stood in the accusation of formula, reason and logic, Nietzsche saw past both worldviews. He saw it at his own personal expense and intended his work to be prophetic notice.

He abandoned his Christianity at a young age to become a "searcher after truth."[6] He called this *having faith*. As theologian Wilfred Cantwell Smith reminds us, Nietzsche does not make his proclamation on a "note of triumph...for Nietzsche, it is an indisputable cultural fact, one which is fraught with the most terrible consequences both for individuals and humanity."[7] He believed that religion made humanity victims of their own imaginations (we see this thinking show up later in the work of Sigmund Freud with religion as 'wish fulfillment') and goes as far as to say that the Christian religion is actually the Anti-Christ and a crime against life.

Raschke reminds us,

> It is clear from Nietzsche's writings that he did not share the Reformation preference for an 'innocent' early version of Christianity...All of Western Christianity had surrendered to the dominance of the democratic state and thereby the values and mentality of the common man, what Nietzsche contemptuously called 'the herd.' The herd craves the metaphysical comfort of God and the moral certainty of theology all bundled up in the popular Platonic fiction of the hereafter.[8]

God was nothing more than fire insurance and what Karl Marx called the "opium of people." And where God was not on life support in society as such, 'he' was gobbled up in the destitute and bankrupt nature of nihilism. There was illusionary meaning, or there was no meaning at all. Both are grim possibilities.

God is, indeed, dead, and we have killed him, echoes the madman. We killed him by creating 'him.' We killed him by containing 'him.' We killed 'him' by stripping the divine of its mystery, experience, and unknowability. We killed 'him' by relying on a myth of our creation when we should have relied on each other and ourselves. It is society and culture that have killed god by venerating god and sacralizing our rituals in the name we have attributed to being; an object of our own construct and, as Nietzsche has asserted, our own imaginations.

F. Leron Shults devotes the opening pages of his book, *Theology After the Birth of God,* to Nietzsche's madman and why nothing has changed in terms of who is listening to his cry. Shults satirically states, "God seems to have survived his death without much difficulty." [9] He contrasts principles taken as gospel to "members of religious coalitions" that say "humans cannot adequately interpret the natural world or appropriately inscribe the social world without help from imagined disembodied intentional forces" with atheism as he defines it: "conceived as an affirmation: yes, we can. Or, at least, we can live trying."[10] Indeed, atheism confronts the theist God, the underlying consciousness and moral God of the ages that holds everything together. However, by confronting the theist God, the post-theist god has been missed, which is what this book and post-Christianity are all about.

DEATH OF GOD, ITS PROPONENTS, AND SURPRISING TRAJECTORY

So, what did the madman culminate in? What does it look like to 'live trying'? As mentioned in my last chapter, April 8, 1966 TIME magazine debuted one of their most iconic, historic, and controversial covers ever,[11] declaring God is dead by declaring in print *Is God Dead?* Stemming from the work of William Hamilton, Thomas Altizer, Paul van Buren and Gabriel Vahanian, Death of God theologians, Radical Theologians, taking off on Nietzsche's "Parable of the Madman" from 1882.

Religious America was up in arms at the brazen and sacrilegious cover. Preachers raged against it on Sundays, hate mail overwhelmed the mailbox of Hamilton, and Altizer received death threats. In an interview with Playboy, even Bob Dylan, a decade later, would criticize the issue, saying, "If you were God, how would you like to see that written about yourself?"[12] This cover seemed to embody Christian America's worst fear; secularization. This was seen as a move away from the Judeo-Christian god that, for many, American values were founded upon and a move toward humanism, secularism, and a host of other 'ungodly' things. This was the sort of public declaration that fueled and gave rise to the Religious Right in America and the Moral Majority movement, including Evangelical and Baptist faith leaders such as Billy Graham, Jerry Falwell, Oral Roberts, Paul Weyrich, and others.

The issue at face value, with little regard to story, interpretation, or context, seemed to be an atheistic pronouncement and an antagonistic one at that. However, this cover and what it was perhaps proclaiming was much more complex and layered than the public gave it credit for. It set in motion a generation of Radical Theology, currently in its fourth wave, that would be a game changer for many Christians, philosophers, and people of faith.

As written about on its 50th anniversary,

> The article was far more nuanced than the cover might suggest, but Hamilton and Altizer were not hedging in their views. It's tempting to take them metaphorically, to say "death" and mean "irrelevance," but they were speaking literally. The idea was not the same as disbelief: God was real and had existed, they said, but had become dead.[13]

The problem was (and is) there were too many instances of hell on earth to believe that a benevolent being, with humanity's best interest at heart, was in charge. At the time of the cover, 97% of Americans said they believed in God. Was it perhaps the construct of this dead God they were holding onto? For better or for worse, was it their only hope?

Bursting this bubble was cause for celebration for Altizer and his colleagues. For them, something was, indeed, combusting! Bursting wide open theological and philosophical constructs that perhaps meant now we could really get somewhere when speaking of religion, meaning, and faith. For them, this was the dawn of a new age filled with promise, hope, and new beginnings.

However, what would unfold with religion over the next several decades up to the present day would not be emancipation of god and faith but a continued entrapment and re-entrenchment into old values and ideologies, clinging to illusions or returning and/or recovering what was lost. Thomas Altizer was to outlive his Death of God colleagues, and in one of his final interviews, he was plainly and painfully dejected at the outcome that had revealed itself through the years. Seeing what he viewed as a dead god continuing to sit on high in Western society and theological thought living mostly at the margins, he admits, "All the things that were crucial to me in the '60s are now gone...I'm not saying this is a bad time, but I think it's a rather empty time—empty of the joy that we once celebrated."[14] What did he mean by this? What disappointed him so much about the trajectory of the movement?

In Altizer and Hamilton's book of essays, *Radical Theology and the Death of God*, which came out around the same time as the 1966 TIME cover, one of the first essays listed, "America and the Future of Theology," Altizer writes, "Observing that the waters of European theology are at present somewhat stagnant, Karl Barth recently said that what we need in Europe and America is not a renewal of an older form of theology but a 'theology of freedom' that looks ahead and strives forward."[15] He goes on to speak of the problem Americans have with understanding the past and present and what that means for the future.

Our country is so young, with no historical monuments to remind us of an age we can boast of. Being unaware of this disadvantage, our imaginations for the future are severely handicapped. Altizer goes on to say, "Thus the American who is in quest of a deeper form of existence must look forward to the future, not a future which is simply an extension of the present, but a future that will shatter all that we know as present...It is precisely such a detachment from the past that may now make possible a new form of theology."[16] As far back as the '60s, the likes of Altizer and Hamilton were professing, "On all sides theologians are agreed that we are now in some sense living in a post-Christian age."[17]

He knew the struggle it would be to give god a new future due to the small, tame, and restrained imaginations of American Christians. He and his colleagues had hoped that this TIME cover would smash a frigid and vapid lack of vision and creativity regarding theology and its impact on society and the future. However, it seems decades later, we are only a little further along to Altizer's great disappointment. Something Nietzsche also predicted, "God is dead; but given the way of men, there may still be caves for thousands of years in which his shadow will be shown. — And we — we still have to vanquish his shadow, too."[18]

Even though in Altizer's opinion, the movement wasn't the success they had hoped for, theological blogger Nathan Smith, while he has his points of departure from Altizer, writes that Altizer was able "to do for the West what many others seemed entirely incapable of doing; to help us learn how to live meaningfully after the death of 'God,' and thus to find *God*."[19] For Altizer, "Nietzsche's proclamation of the death of god gave witness to the advent of a new historical moment. This moment transformed transcendence into immanence, thereby dissolving the religious ground of subjectivity and inwardness."[20]

This is precisely what we can credit the Death of God movement with; shattering a particular construct of god so that we may be free to explore a future of faith that will be marked by a search for god, that, unlike its predecessors, will have no destination, no arrival, no finish. It will be marked by a spiral that keeps us engaged, makes us better, more deeply and fully human, and allows us to continue in our search for meaning with the Christian narrative at the heart of that search.

Altizer sought to bring awareness for how god was employed in society, and in the '60s, just a few decades after WWII, concentration camps, Hiroshima, in the throes of the Vietnam conflict, Civil Rights, communism, and assassinations everywhere one turned, there had to be a 'man behind the curtain' moment to reveal that there was nothing behind the curtain at all. But, again, not to be misinterpreted as an atheistic statement. It was a declaration that we had been revering in the wrong direction.

In a 1968 interview with Alec Gilmore, Altizer spoke practically about what the Death of God movement means for society and the common person. Gilmore closes the conversation with this final question, "What do you see now to be the future development of the death of God theology? Be a prophet and look forward and tell me what might happen." Altizer's reply,

Of course, I don't know. I am not a prophet. I have no vision of the future. But I think it is already clear that what we know as traditional Christian theology has had its day and will only live among reactionary groups; they may perpetuate themselves in a sectarian form but that will be all. Instead I think we shall get a substantially new form of theology, a new form of faith, a new form of worship, and a new form of community.[21]

More than half a century later, we still yearn for this new faith. And precisely because it has yet to come into fruition is why we have seen the 97% of 1966 drop to 63% in 2015, and it continues to decline. God needs to mean something more than punitive judge or wet noodle. The narrative has to be powerful yet resonate with what it means to be human, our histories, stories, and community. We need to make meaning out of our experiences, and we need to see the transformative effects not only in our lives but in the lives of those around us. If we don't, then we are simply not interested.

Post-Christian thought seeks to make room for not only the glaringly absent cultural components we find in churches and Christianity but also a faith that can be articulated while also at peace and resolve in the only thing life promises, uncertainty. If god after the Death of God has a future at all, it will be given one because of all the failings of the present state of affairs of Christianity in the West.

RADICAL THEOLOGY AND THE FUTURE

Where are we after God's death? After the likes of Franco Berardi telling us that our future has been blown to bits, after the resurgence of fundamental religious values, and the racist affairs of 20th-century Evangelicalism that further diseased American Christianity? Where are we after our god(s) have flailed and failed? Well, you are here.

Reading this book. Because you suspect there might be a future where your faith can live, thrive, evolve, and really mean something. And you are right to suspect this. You are right to follow your curiosities, your suspicions, your wonderings and wanderings, your doubts, and all the whispers that have been loyal to you, and to *event*, and to the only thing to which all loyalty points—the *undeconstrible*.

John Caputo says that "The real interest of theology is not in God. At the end of the day, it is in the best interests of theology not to be content with God. Theology has other interests."[22] But what else could theology possibly be concerned with if not 'God?' For Caputo and others, theology is about having "deeper interests" than simply the God on high. If theology is only interested in what Caputo calls "the Supreme Being, the highest being of them all", then this is "high theology" concerned with a most high God. This is the God who is dead, who has died. The God of metaphysics, the Big Other in the sky; the interventionist God who does not actually intervene.

What opposes such "high theology?" For Caputo, the answer is "weak theology." The search for a god that goes deep rather than high; that is weak as opposed to strong. This "deep theology," as Caputo refers to it, is known as "radical theology, meaning getting down in the dirt and digging down into the roots of theology."[23] Caputo takes off on Paul's words in 1 Corinthians 1:25 "because the folly of God is wiser than humans are and the weakness of God is stronger than human are." Caputo succinctly and poignantly sums up radical theology as "where there is height, I head for the depth; where there is a show of strength, I prefer weakness. Instead of high and might, we radical theologians seek the deep and weak!"[24]

Radical theology is about a reorientation to how we speak and think about god and, better yet, all that is being done and housed in its name. It means rethinking everything you thought you knew about *God in the highest*. The God that demands worship and commands the utmost control. The God who smites all his (and your) enemies. It is about removing ourselves from the safe and illusionary confines of certainty and opening ourselves up to all that might be, or as Caputo puts it, "in the coming of what we cannot see coming."[25]

Radical theology flies in the face of confessional theology. Whereas confessional theology seeks to declare all we know God to be, radical theology seeks to declare all that we know not of god. But not in some mystical way in which god is in everything and everywhere, in various forms of pantheism and/or panentheism. But in a way that haunts us, that whispers to us of all that might be. A still small voice, perhaps, that taunts us, disrupts and interrupts us. It somehow begins to alert us to the dream that the possible is even more stunningly impossible, and that what we believe we know is actually past the bounds of knowledge. It whispers to us that what we have conditioned has no conditions and is in fact unconditional, and that what we have named, tamed, and domesticated is unnameable, untamable, and is savagely wild. Haphazard, yet elegant. Unpredictable as the echoes of its howling leaves us searching for its next move, which we can never anticipate. To be loyal to such a specter, speaking of the apophatic, as we wait for apparition, which has already come and gone but is on its way again and which we won't know is back until it is upon us and will leave as quickly as it arrived.

It all sounds so exciting. And it is, indeed. But it is also life as it truly is. Uncertain, no guarantees, no center, no holy grail that will answer all of life's precarities and peculiarities. The phantom asks us to have faith in more by believing less. A faith that will invite us deeper into our own humanity, asking for rebirth every day, as we join the charge that has always been to make things new. This is traveling *safer than the known way.*

I think this is why I passed liberal forms of Christianity right by in terms of a faith home. Because while the theology is infinitely more bearable than that of its conservative Evangelical counterparts, the constructs are still the same. There is God-but this God is nice. And while it was attractive in some ways at the time, I just knew I had to heed the whispers and keep going. Off the edge, into the unknown, and whatever would be would be, whatever would come would come. It was my desire, and for me, the unknown was safer. There was peace about it all.

I remember when these theological changes were well underway in my life. Changes I was excited about, that started to make sense of some things for me, and that I found healing and transformative. I still hadn't quite shaken the little Evangelist in me, which meant I was happy to share about all I was learning, and all that was happening. I learned very quickly that this sort of theological outlook and rhetoric was not welcome in circles that I thought were safe. I gave the Evangelicalism of those I loved and were close to too much credit. I had to learn some lessons the hard way, but in the end, it helped me establish clear boundaries and reset expectations of how much of my life and faith I was willing to lay bare. Of course, this is dependent on the theological lens and held beliefs of those that one is speaking with. I was once asked in a most definitive way if I found I had more peace in my life and if all was well with my soul when no one was around (the implication being away from my fancy theological circles). The answer was an unhesitant "yes," to which the reply was "I don't believe you."

It was an unfortunate moment. It was painful then and now. But my answer to that apparently unanswerable question is as true now as it was then. I have found such peace and comfort in releasing my ever-so-tight grip on all that I thought I knew to be true about God. In following the curiosity that apparently killed the cat, having been led to the death of the highest order, I became free from all (un)holy constraints. Living in pursuit and in hope of all that may (or may not) usher in the end of liberation. There is no more to be set free from. I have been set free from it all, and I can't help but be reminded of a very familiar line of Scripture, "So if the Son sets you free, you will be free indeed" (John 8:36). Perhaps Jesus had his own death of God moment on the cross, "my God, my God, why have you forsaken me?" (Mark 15:34). Slavoj Žižek calls this a moment of atheism for Christ.[26]

In Paul Hessert's, *Christ and the End of Meaning*, he proposes that god lives "in the absence of meaning and power"[27] and that the act of the cross was the end of meaning, the end of certainty. Hessert writes as he prepares to introduce his readers to scandal,

> The Gospel as we have it from St. Paul and the Evangelists, however, proclaims Christ crucified, messiah slain—and invites hearers to join Christ in his Passion. In that break with the culture's circle of reality, where power fails and meaning dissolves, God who is neither the culture's creation nor its legitimator opens the reality of faith—living in the absence of meaning and power.[28]

"It is finished." A small phrase that packs a big punch, but not because of sin and death and heaven and hell, and all the other baggage we were told it meant. But because of the reality of freedom at the most primal of levels! An immunity to the tempting and illicit offer that life and its pangs can be figured out unto reward and an opportunity to be released from all that we have been compelled to be beholden by. It is all a mouth full, I know. To be honest, there is no easy way to speak of it. Not only will language always fall short but more importantly, language cannot keep up. Yet we try. This is why radical theology is a way of speaking apophatically about god, a way of negating all that we have traditionally accepted about God. I have used apophatic terms throughout this volume and will continue to as our words can do nothing more than their best attempt to allude to our phenomenal experiences. Caputo refers to this beautifully and poetically as "wounded language."[29]

If there is a stand-alone intent in any of this (as opposed to negated intent), it can perhaps be understood as having a goal with no goalposts, sailing towards a horizon with no line, and just maybe a compass that doesn't point north.

To return again to the work and words of Jeffrey Robbins, he speaks of radical theology as a way that "transforms what it means to think theologically."[30] He says it "leads us to the seemingly impossible possibility of a theology after the death of God, between faith and suspicion and stripped bare of its appeal to religion, supernaturalism, and mythology. To be sure, this is a theology unrecognizable to most."[31] He goes on to say,

It is neither theistic nor atheistic but still recognizes God as a formulation of extremity that gets *at the root* of thought and opens up pathways for a thinking that *knows no bounds*. In this way, the idea of God and the desire for God outlive the death of God, and thus, although radical theology emerged out of the death-of-god moment, it is no longer bound by that movement.[32]

While it started with Nietzsche and his madman, TIME and its cover, Altizer and Hamilton, et al., it does not and has not ended there.

Caputo talks about exposing confessional theology to "instability and the instability goes all the way down...That is the disturbance."[33] He goes on to say, "The disturbance constitutes the stuff of radical theology, requiring an unnerving faith that runs deeper than the reassuring beliefs..."[34] This is what we are after! "Unnerving faith" instead of "reassuring beliefs!"[35] This is where transformation occurs! This is where we choose bravery and courage as we forge into the night without light and walk *safer than the known way*.

We get to the root of the quest. We go deep down into the underbelly of this whole thing as we find the search is in and of itself theological. That we vow not to be distracted by the flash of the high God with all its promises of fulfillment and finery. That we push past the allure and cache of the God of glory and strength. That we look right through the fanciful and faithless nature of the God of omniscience, omnipresence, and omnipotence, and we live past it, through it, and in spite of it. Not as one who rebels but as one which revels. Reveling in and ravelling towards a future of a most radical nature for which there is no substitute.

A future of faith—your future and mine—for which there will be no compromise.

5

DECONSTRUCTION THEN, NOW, AND AS IT MAY BE TO COME, PERHAPS

"Viens, Oui, oui."[1]

— **Jackie Derrida**

PARIS, DEATH, AND DERRIDA

This past summer, I found myself in Paris for the umpteenth time. When I was younger, Paris was one of those fairytale places little American girls dream about. It is perhaps what seems to be over the rainbow. Before you realize it is a real city, with sounds and smells, trash and tragedy. All you see in your mind's eye is all the movies have ever shown you. The glitzy and glimmering Eiffel Tower, romantic boat rides along the Seine, the bells of Notre Dame, the sizzle of crepes, the hissing of espresso, the crying of the accordion. I wanted it all. Yet I didn't have it until my 30th birthday. It was the last big thing my ex-husband and I did together before our separation.

I knew very little of France. I had never been there, yet I dreamed of living there. To be honest, I dreamed of living anywhere beautiful that would remove me from the painful situation I found myself in. I very much wanted to escape. And Paris has had her arms open wide to emotional refugees like me for centuries. After a week of seeing so much of what people went to see, I was taken with the city that had not lost its luster.

I have long wanted to go to the grave of Jacques Derrida, which resides outside of Paris in the southern suburb of Ris-Orangis. Although I am not a grave visiting sort of person. I have been to several famous cemeteries throughout Europe because of their beauty and notoriety. Not so much to visit a particular grave. My upbringing did not value visiting the dead and visiting their final resting places, no matter who they were, and I never valued it either. But there was just something that was calling me to visit the grave of Derrida. When you are a theologian or an academic, or even a practitioner of various philosophical ways of understanding the world, so many of one's "mentors" are dead. Are there living scholars that I have gleaned much from? Of course! You have read for yourself so many within the pages of this book already. But then there are those whose work, lives, ways of being in the world, and very existence unequivocally changes everything for everyone. This was Jacques Derrida. Or as he was born and what is imprinted in weatherworn gold into a marble slab, *Jackie Derrida*.

I decided to do something I don't think I've ever attempted to do, make a pilgrimage. I have never used that word in my life to describe anything I have done. And I'm not sure when I will again. I have been quite against flocking to geographic locations that are supposed to be more holy or more sacred than others, when I firmly believe in the utter blurring of the lines between the sacred and profane. Also, I don't appreciate the theological implications of holy places on earth. It bleeds, no, it hemorrhages into supernatural realities that I no longer trade in. But here I was making a pilgrimage and was only too happy to acquiesce to this avoided experience to the resting place of Jackie Derrida.

I found myself being drawn to visit the grave of someone I have never met yet have been so impacted by. Simon and I drove to a run-of-the-mill suburb of Paris to try and find his grave. We eventually found the grave in the beating, hot sun. No breeze. No wind. It was a heatwave in Europe. The perfect time to search for a grave with no shade. My husband left once we found it, respectfully, to leave me to do whatever it is I wanted to do graveside. I preferred to be alone there, and he knew that.

The issue is I didn't know what I wanted to do or say. As I stood there in the hot sun, it hit me, "Ok, now what?" What did I really hope to accomplish here? What did I want to say? What did I want to do? How did I want to feel? I can tell you how I didn't want to feel. I didn't want to feel stupid. But I did a little. At that moment, sweating my brains out in the boiling sun, visiting the grave of a complete stranger, who I know very little about, I felt stupid. I also felt like an intruder.

I was not family, and I was not a friend, and here I was at someone's final resting place. Maybe I didn't even belong there. But, in any case, I was there and so I better make the most of it. I took some pictures of his very plain grave, the one he shares with his wife. It was a long slab of marble with their names and dates, and that was it. No headstone. No monuments or statues. No "here lies beloved father, husband, son, etc." Quite unassuming and without ceremony or any of the pomp and circumstance you would expect for such a colossus.

There I was. I decided to speak some words to the dust. In my self-perceived foolishness of talking to a grave, as well as feeling a little bit of shame for encroaching on a perhaps sacred spot (despite my denial that such places exist, I think I would have to concede that we as humans make places holy if there is hallowed ground to be trodden) as an uninvited guest, I spoke out just the same.

I told him that he most likely has no idea I'm here, and if he does, then he probably doesn't care anyway. And that probably no one is listening, but since I'm here, let me just say this...

I proceeded to tell him what his work has meant for me. How I imagine he might have felt in his early life, about what he had become (even though he was a formidable scholar when he died), and what his work continues to mean to the world.

I shed a few tears at the injustice of death and the injustice of life. The loneliness we can often feel, the way we can be outliers in our own existence, and how we are all just desperate for some kind of take-your-breath-away moment to live on until we are lucky enough to be visited by such a phenomenon once more. In many ways, this is what 'event' was for Derrida. But I wonder if he knew he *was* event? That he was the force that changed everything for everyone. His critics read him logically, which is an inappropriate way to handle his work. His proponents read him wonder-fully, thinking they have his thought mastered and feel liberated by it. But like the ghosts he often spoke of, and like event made us aware of, he cannot be reasoned with, mastered by, relegated to, or reckoned with. He was such a skilful and gifted thinker, an artist of thought and interpretation, and a craftsman and composer of insight and intelligence.

THE WAGER OF PERHAPS, THE PROMISE OF EVENT

I have made much mention of this idea of *event*. I remember when I first heard the term, event, used in a theological context. It went something like this, "God is event and experience, as opposed to being and object." I would sit there and take in statements like this. I would nod my head and feel the excitement of theological resonance and radicality. My mind was engrossed, awake and alert to all that was moving towards me. I could grasp some of it, and some I couldn't. I understood what they meant to say when employing terms like *being* and *object*. This refers to the ontology of God; the empirical, metaphysical reality of God. But experience sounded too obviously post-modern that it couldn't quite be that. And, event? What was this?

I have used it here, up until now, with no explanation in order for you to become hopefully a bit curious. To start to imagine what it might mean given how it's used in context. To maybe be mystified by it. To inspire questions about it. To even be enchanted by it, as I was and still am. And, also, because to speak of event is impossible. As stated earlier, language is always our best attempt. But since the *impossible* is what we want, let's have at it.

The idea of the event is the philosophical language that Derrida uses, taking off from the work of Martin Heidegger. Heidegger describes event (as if it could be) with the following:

> The event is experienced in pliancy toward the dispensa-
> tion into the twisting free out of which Da-sein [German
> for 'being there' or 'presence'/often translated in English
> as existence] essentially occurs, in which guise the totality
> of beyng is. The thinking of the history of beyng [being
> but as event and the non-metaphysical way to speak of
> being] is the venture of saying the unsayable without
> naming it. Even the "beginning" and the event are only
> forewords. The resonance is thus the clearing voice of the
> stillness.[2]

Now, you can see why these sorts of concepts perhaps never properly make it to pop culture, where they could be really powerful. Because, really, who has time to get their brains tongue-tied like this? It is quite difficult to understand and even more difficult to find useful employ-ment of its ideas. But, but, but, but(!), if we can somehow find the patience and grace to exist in a realm where we can suspend our frus-trations, our impatience, and our intolerance towards non-immediate mastery, we may find ourselves beautifully surprised and humbled at what might occur. And it is (im)possibly this, that when we speak of being the conclusion of the metaphysical was either too early or too late. Does this still sound like you're a guest at the Mad Hatter's tea party? Good. Then you're reading it correctly.

These sorts of concepts ask us to do the undoable. Which is going back before our memory, both personal and historical, to a mode of thinking that asks stillness of us to confront such stillness alone. What we encounter there is not to be spoken of. It is unsayable and impossible, but it requires a willingness to accept what it means to be human. This is what we discover in the unsayable; the human condition, and it is unspeakably stunning. We even locate the unsayability of being and event of god.

This is why moving towards a post-Christian understanding is so vital for the faith of the future, and our faith presently for that matter! It is not about silencing what has been said of God, but humility in knowing we can only say these things about god, *perhaps*.

Derrida picks up on this language of event and appropriates it within the trendy philosophical climate of French structuralism of the mid and latter half of the 20th century. Derrida was a philosopher, not a theologian. Although many would call him a theologian of sorts. He was a non-religious French Algerian Jew and was often quoted as saying he "quite rightly passed for an atheist."[3]

I will invite us again to turn the clocks back to 1966. But this time, not April, the month the infamous TIME magazine article was published, but October. Jacques Derrida is virtually unknown at 36 years old. A French philosophy teacher, he takes the stage at a conference on structuralism at John Hopkins University to present a paper entitled "Structure, Sign and play in the Discourse of Human Sciences." All the heavy hitters were there. Derrida was a last-minute invite after someone had canceled. He was quiet most of the conference in the midst of presenters like Hans-Georg Gadamer and Jacques Lacan and didn't speak until the final day, in the final session, for the final hour.

Now for quick background, the philosophical concept known as structuralism replaced existentialism. Existentialism was about the free subject. It was human-centered, particular, and individual. Structuralism says that the only way we can understand anything is by understanding it in relationship to the wider structure of its context, what it is a part of, and what it is in relation to. Everything is part of a schema, and that relationship needs to be examined and understood before we can make sense of the actual thing we are investigating.

This was applied to many disciplines and fields, not least of which literature, as it was being understood as part of larger narratives, shared horizons, and arcs rather than (empirical/actual) authorial intention alone. It was groundbreaking and exciting for many. However, like most things, rules were made, and guidelines set. Interesting that a framework that was supposed to liberate meaning from a former framework had now re-entrenched itself within another system of boundaries. It was co-opted and caged. It is surprising how often this happens.

So, Derrida. Final speaker, final day, final session. He starts, as his recent biographer Peter Salmon reminds us,

"Perhaps something has occurred in the history of the concept of structure that could be called an 'event.'"[4]

While Salmon indicates Derrida spoke for less than 30 minutes, by the time he was finished, "the entire structuralist project was in doubt, if not dead. An event had occurred: the birth of deconstruction."[5]

Derrida knew there were caveats. There were things that could not be explained, experiences that would blow apart our epistemologies and everything we ever thought we knew. There would be moments that would cause us to question everything, and there would be movement in our lives that defied the directions we thought possible.

Event ruins everything in a really good way.

But we must leave room for it, even though there is no way to expect it. Because if we expect it, that means we have a precedent for it, which we don't. Because if we do, or if we model it on something that has already occurred, then it is not event. It is simply just more of the same.

I think many of us miss event because we are too busy expecting what we know to expect, what we have experienced before, what we long for again, and what we can track with and return to. It is a good enough life, being sure of such things. It is safe and comfortable, and there is nothing wrong with that. I am not a naysayer when it comes to being comfortable and doing what we know. I have my routines and my traditions and experiences I will always come back to. But it is my best and most earnest dream to know event. To be caught up by its haunting, as it comes at me from the future, colliding with the past and making for a present moment that is gone as fast as I can experience it. That it would teach me something new about myself, the world, what it means to be human, and more about this meaning-making we call god. This I want in my life more than anything.

Deconstruction is the understanding that there is a sense of innate self-destruction in what we engage. Meaning that it can combust with event at any time. It is the secret built into structure and into all things, the moment of deconstruction. Subject to deconstruction is our god(s), religion, faith understanding, the way we read scripture, church, experiences, and the like. Realizing this and understanding this is the first step to engaging what true deconstruction is. It is not a phenomenon, it is expected, developed, and presented on a cultural and historical plain. The uncovering of this reality allows us to be open to event and to have the honorable response; zero anticipation and expectancy, yet forever changed until it visits us once more (which it is always doing if we allow for it). And rather than give you long philosophical prose about deconstruction and post-structuralism, I mostly want to spike your interest for all that is coming that you cannot see coming. That if you pray, to encourage you to pray for event. That it would disrupt you and disentangle you from all you think you know, to invite you to something other and something else.

Deconstruction is an allowance innate in all things. We should search it out wherever it is to be found. But we must know that the only thing deconstruction is loyal to is the Undeconstructible. I have spoken of this a few times, although I have not defined it. Because it is undefinable. It is the Impossible, it is the Unconditional. It is the hope and history of 'beyng.' Without memory, without remembrance, as it is that which cannot be remembered and that which cannot be recollected. Da-sein; presence without being, existence without meta-physics. It is our humanity, alone in the dark, awakening to the "voice of stillness." The voice which does not speak and the presence which does not make itself known until it is gone, but still there, but gone again.

This flipped upside down way of speaking. This talk of everything and nothing. Is it the only possible way to speak of the Impossible? In a way that seems to convey nothing and also all things? This ever on the move, elusive (non/a)presence?

Derrida spent his career attempting to speak of it all in a word, 'l'avenir.' The French word for 'to come.' Only it wasn't just about an arrival; it was a nuance, a mutual understanding between us and the Impossible—to be open to all that we cannot see coming, but shall come indeed. L'avenir is an event. It is coming, and it is going at the same time. It cannot be regulated or commanded, nor can it be pinned down. It escapes philosophy, theology, and language, for that matter, yet we are haunted by it and its (non/a)presence. The moment we try to define it or think we have it covered, it moves on yet comes to us also. A quandary for some, misunderstood as a labyrinth by most, but it is the permeating and puncturing force of our lives.

L'avenir. 'To come.' But not in a far-off, futuristic way or in a way we can plan for or see coming on the horizon. The French have a word for that sort of understanding of the future...le futur. No. L'avenir is imminent. It is the coming of the future, but also the arrival of it at the same time. L'avenir is not an epic arrival, it is not an event with a beginning and ending point. It has zero possibility of being denied, it is entirely other (wholly other/tout autre), and it will always escape attempts of mastery and containment. It isn't even a moment. It is a signal. A signal that "unhinges" and "disjoints"[6] the movement in question and provokes understanding, but in part. This spin around us. It is exciting! It signals to us that something is on the move and always so! As Jean-Paul Martinon writes, "Avenir signals that something is afoot."[7] Indeed, it is!

When something like l'avenir exists, or insists, how can empirical knowledge also exist? What are our boxes, categories, and paradigms in the face of l'avenir? What are our proud theologies, full of perfect knowledge, hubris and our god(s) in the roars and whispers and teasing and taunts of l'avenir?

It is the cue that we don't actually know all that we think we do, and it is the wink that says we never will.

Derrida knew there were caveats to all things. So, what is the caveat he put among his work and suspected may be in all things? His inquisition and inquiry? Well, *perhaps*. Talk about saying something with a wink! It drove his harshest critics mad with the unfounded nature and chaos of it all and gathered to him fanfare from the bourgeois of nuance. As Carl Raschke writes, "Because Derrida in both profile and profession shattered every conceivable mould, he became an object of both reverence and derision."[8] But what was maybe missed by the lot of them was his *perhaps* was an utterance of indication of the whereabouts of his loyalty. To the Undeconstructible, taking up in his own most ardent dreams and imaginations of l'avenir. Indeed, whatever he might have said, whatever you might have said about whatever he might have said, it's over now and has been handed over to *perhaps*.

John Caputo rightly admits, "There is every reason for philosophers and theologians to fear this small word, 'perhaps.'"[9] He explains it this way,

> "Perhaps" is the only way to say yes to the future... "Perhaps" is thus a non-knowing... "Perhaps" is not a simple disinterest but a word of desire for something, I know not what, something I desire with a "desire beyond desire"..."Perhaps" is not to be confused with the "possible" as the counterpart of the actual, with a merely logical possibility or empirical unpredictability..."Perhaps" gives us access to something that eludes the rule of knowledge as certainty and method because it belongs

to another register..."Perhaps" sounds like the soul of indecision, like a lame excuse for an answer, a refusal to take a stand, the safest course "possible." I, on the other hand, think it is risky business, a venture into the abyss, a wild and disproportionate risk, exposing us to an excess, opening us to the best while exposing us to the worst, deprived of the mighty armor of metaphysics.[10]

He goes on to say,

> "Perhaps" sounds like it has renounced all truth and has consigned itself to a regime of opinion. But in truth the society of the friends of "perhaps" is also the society of the true friends of truth, not because they are *in* the truth, which means inside the secure confines of certainty and dogma, but in the sense of befriending it, seeking it, loving it, exposing themselves to its unforeseeable and dangerous coming, to the risk of the "perhaps."[11]

DECONSTRUCTION AND POP CULTURE

I think it is really important to introduce Derrida and deconstruction, the subverting weak yet haunting force of l'avenir, and the hope of perhaps in a book like this one. Especially, given the current climate of exodus en masse from Christianity that is going by the term deconstruction. It is important to share language and have collective and meaningful ways of talking about our experiences that we can create community around. Yet, at the same time, Derrida's deconstruction is so moving; it shoots across the sky, infusing and electrifying everything in its path and preparing us for that which we cannot prepare for but instead can only "call 'come.'"[12]

Deconstruction, at a pop culture level, is used to denote the experience of leaving fundamental and usually Evangelical circles of Christianity. Deconstruction has become a synonym for disentangling and disentwining from toxic forms of religion and belief. Over the last few years, it has become a term that leaders from the religious right have denounced as demonic. They have done their best to co-opt the term in order to try and control the process they saw unfolding before their eyes. In fact, almost two years ago, The Gospel Coalition published a book on deconstruction to try and buy back the doubt with a mix of manipulation, fear, and bad theology known to them as *truth*. Quoir, the publisher of this book, put out a rebuttal[13] within a month of which I am a contributor.

I have spoken with my colleagues over the last few years about how exactly this term was made to mean all it has taken on as of late. With no reflection of Heidegger, Derrida, or Caputo. In fact, about a year ago, I had a podcast conversation with Jack Caputo, along with Barry Taylor. I asked Jack if he knew that the term had become so popular and informed him how it was used. He had no knowledge of deconstruction being spoken of in this manner and asked if I could send him some examples.

The current dialogue on deconstruction is being mostly had online via social media platforms, and it is a vitriolic one, no matter which side of the spectrum you might be on. And I get it. A whole generation of people who invested their time, money, energy, relationships, and, in short, their lives in a form of Christianity that used and abused them are now starting to see what they couldn't see before. And that is, at the very least, that Western Christianity (and Western Christianity's God) simply cannot deliver on its promises. And, depending on one's church or denominational affiliation, there have been varying degrees of trauma, manipulation, abuse, exploitation, profiteering, and control that continue to be exposed. In a sense, the vitriol is well deserved. But in another sense, it keeps an open wound open, festering with infection without a way to heal.

There is a lot of talk of religious trauma among these sorts of deconstruction circles. New fields of therapy are being pursued and researched. More accountability is demanded from institutions and leaders that have gotten away with far too much for far too long. The Christian understanding of God is now being expanded to *Universe*, *Love*, and a host of other nouns that are bigger, kinder, more forgiving, and more mysterious than all we know 'God' to have been.

There seems to be so much that people are equating with this notion. Are religious trauma and deconstruction the same? Is moving from conservative Christianity to progressive Christianity equivalent to deconstruction? Is a lightbulb moment of one's initial thoughts of doubt the beginning of deconstruction?

First, let me say this. If one genuinely feels one has experienced trauma, religious or otherwise, one needs to find a good therapist specializing in that kind of specific trauma. This is not to be minimized in any way. Secondly, if crimes have been committed and laws have been broken, this must be pursued in a court of law. Legal action should be taken, and people must be held accountable. It is essential to distinguish between mental health and psychological conditions, criminal activity and theological movements and shifts that are occurring. I have seen these pieces get conflated and needs not be met appropriately.

The current community claiming the term deconstruction is quite opposed to anyone defining the term as they have designated it. However, when we are talking about deconstruction as a theological movement, we must be honest about some things. In the aftermath of this particular deconstruction, another kind of belief is reconstructed. It is usually either a more liberated, inclusive Jesus and/or God, or in some cases, agnosticism/atheism, with lots of memes, sarcasm, disdain, and contempt along the way. The issue here is that it is all still on a sliding scale of traditional notions of being and agency, and all one is doing is reacting to whatever else might be on that sliding scale.

Those currently 'deconstructing' are finding more palatable ways of engaging faith that they either don't want to throw away or engage it by raging against it. Both are understandable. The issue is neither is deconstruction. If we are serious about deconstruction and if we genuinely want to be radical enough to hop the aforementioned sliding scale, then indeed, deconstruction is what we are after, but not as it currently is. There is so much to say about true deconstruction, as we have only begun to scratch the surface. As John Caputo has written with caution and a certain type of reverence, "'Doing deconstruction,' if deconstruction is something to do, is not a matter of the very latest, up-to-date, ahead-of-itself, *avant-garde*, postmodern one-upmanship. Deconstruction has to do with the oldest of the old as well as with what is coming."[14]

In chapter one, I talked about the moment in the South of France when I first read the words and work of Mark C. Taylor and his indictment upon circles. That was over several years ago now. At the time, there was no term for those who found themselves smack-dab in the middle of what I can only retroactively describe as faith transition. As explained, it started some years before that moment, and I had no idea what to call it, what was happening, or where I might end up. There were many who were 'losing faith' or joining the ranks of a more 'progressive' or 'liberal' understanding of Christianity. Still, this word, *deconstruction*, as it is used today, was not available to pop culture in this way quite yet.

There were no models to follow, there weren't a ton of books available or language created to address this journey I was on. It would take me many years to gather up and create the language that I needed to talk about this process, which was ultimately a demythologizing and deconverting experience. Eventually, I had shed the pressure of trying to figure it all out and had somehow made peace with the haunting. This haunting that lead me away but not unto just yet, which would have been the destination anyway; *unto not just yet.*

The current conversation on deconstruction is an interesting one. I have sat back and taken some time to listen to it closely. I'm not even sure 'deconstruction' is the best term for it all. Perhaps it is more of a devaluing of things we once valued, devolving into something else that is evolving. Within the deconstruction movement today, there seems to be an exchange happening. A deconstructing of sorts in order to reconstruct its counterpart that we like better and a way of talking about theological matters that are still deceptively modern, speaking in terms of false binaries.

For example, because Scripture is no longer accepted as inerrant and infallible, it is now simply a historical document filled with mistakes, multiple authors, and stories of Jesus and the early church in which no (and far from it) original documents can be accessed. It is full of mistakes, historical slip-ups, empirical no-shows, and lacks the facticity words like *inerrancy* and *infallibility* claim. So, the bible has been debunked, and a favorite 'gotcha' moment of atheism has been lived out again. But this conversation is a total snooze in both directions and doesn't get us anywhere. But it is possible, and more than that necessary, to talk about authority and scripture in a way that releases it from the seemingly two options of simply being *true* or not. We can speak about it in a way that gives it all a bit more movement and plasticity. This is the conversation I'm interested in, and I would dare to say is part of what it means to have a post-Christian conversation. Because even the atheist conversation is a Christian one. We must be post those categories to get any traction.

This is what happens when we exchange belief for faith. Belief tells us that we have to choose a side, then we have to choose a category, and it presents us with acceptable options that fall somewhere on the theist/atheist spectrum. But it doesn't get us anywhere. Not only that, but it also leaves a lot of brokenness in its wake. These are the types of circles we must put a stop to if we are to have the post-Christian conversation and if faith is to be engaged further into the future.

Part of what I think is a healthy deconstruction process (if we are going to call it that) is to first and foremost understand that you are about to answer an invitation from a ghost, from a whisper. It is one that beckons you towards a reality of uncertainties. If we are to dismantle or deconstruct anything, it must first be our addiction to certainty. If we can do this we will be free to blow past categories of existence. Language like objective, metaphysical, supernatural will no longer be a concern. Binaries like literal vs. nonliteral, inerrant vs. errant, fact vs. fiction, being vs. non-being become obsolete. These things simply won't matter anymore.

Philosophies that need to account for god and religion in the non-literal sense become superfluous and irrelevant, and our faith becomes free to pursue god, life, and our humanity outside of classifications of certainty and assuredness, no matter how *blessed* that *assurance* may be. Gianni Vattimo talks about how when god is no longer synonymous with metaphysicality we can believe again. When we become aware that "the vision of being as...objectivist metaphysical is untenable, we are left with the biblical notion of creation."[15]

Engaging a sense of faith in my life has little to do with belief. The discomfort with this word and the concept of belief has been years in the making. My faith, and my engagement with it, isn't based on what I believe and what I don't believe. Rather than focus on the belief in or of something, I much prefer to soak deep down into the theological journey faith might take us on if we can liberate ourselves from the entanglement of belief. Belief harasses and maligns faith. They are not the same, and often belief is the enemy of faith. It keeps it static and immovable. It keeps it in a circle with no plausible or possible way to go. When we remove belief, the same way when we bypass existence and being, we can open up the categories for faith, god, religion, and meaning in ways that are endless and boundless, and in ways that *belief* can only dream of!

In Julia Kristeva's *The Incredible Need to Believe*, she names such a need as "neither more nor less than the history of humanity: the speaking being is a believing being."[16] This is her answer to the question of human belief from a secular point of view. Not merely relegated to religious mechanisms of knowing and claiming. From a humanity standpoint, we desire to know, we crave to believe, and we hunger for the security it brings. A temptation of the flesh of the most primal order.

She closes out her thoughts by stating that there is a call "not for a return *to* but a refoundation *of* the authority of the Greco-Judeo-Christianity that gave the world the desire for a 'common world'...It is up to us to reinterpret this gift."[17] It isn't about belief. It is about reinterpreting, reimagining, reconstituting, and refiguring. It is a gift. All of it. We sense this, surely. This is why certain brands of belief are being raged against by the current pop culture 'deconstruction' community.

The deconstruction conversation happening at the moment is all about change. It's changing away from a context and a construct that no longer has its integrity intact. This change and shift is the evidence of having moved through and survived something quite profound.

There is meaning beyond metaphysicality, there is life beyond certainty, and faith beyond belief. Spooked by ghosts returning from the past and coming at us from the future, whispering *no more circles*, it is untenable to stay the same. When we deconstruct, we don't do it along a continuum, we do it deep and down into the abyss, where certainty is condemned as myth and fairytale (and nightmare!), mystery is a tenet to live by, and we measure our meaning-making mechanisms, like god and religion, by their ability to be life-affirming. The risk is great, but if paradigms can be shifted and expectations subverted and turned upside down, you will find yourself hopping the track of the circle and living more deeply and integrally human than you ever thought possible because the impossible is what we are now after.

So, the question is, are we brave enough for actual deconstruction?

It is a confronting and discomforting wager, the coming of the Impossible. But it was Derrida's wager. It is the true wager deconstruction asks us to make; the desire for the *tout autre*, the wholly other. Yet if we desire the wholly other, then "we do not know what we desire," In fact, "We are all dreaming of an absolute surprise, pondering an absolute secret, all waiting of the *tout autre* to arrive."[18]

This is deconstruction; the coming of the waiting and the waiting of the coming of all that is wholly other, which of course, is all that is impossible. Possible has failed, failed unambiguously and miserably.

Caputo writes, "the business of deconstruction is not to police theologians or anybody else...But to keep things open." He continues, "deconstruction is not out to undo God or deny faith, or to mock science or make nonsense of literature...Deconstruction is rather the thought, if it is a thought, of an absolute heterogeneity that unsettles all the assurances of the same within which we comfortably ensconce ourselves."[19]

Are we courageous enough to approach the coming of the impossible with an openness that will "unsettle all the assurances"[20] of all that we have ever known, surrounded ourselves with, and believed in?

This is the deconstruction wager of *perhaps* and the promise of *event*. One that is not accepted lightly, and one we find chooses us as much as we think we choose it.

Are we ready to take the wager?

Are we ready to leave the sliding scale in our dust?

Are we ready to have the post-Christian conversation in pursuit of all that is next?

I join John Caputo in his desire, "I dream of learning how to say 'perhaps.'"[21] Maybe you do too. Let's travel *safer than the known way* and make the dream a reality.

6

A THEOLOGICAL IMAGINATION FOR THE FUTURE

"The anatheist moment is one available to anyone who experience instants of deep disorientation, doubt, or dread, when we are no longer sure exactly who we are or where we are going."[1]

— **Richard Kearney**

FAITH AFTER FAITH AND FAITH BEYOND BELIEF

I FIRST ENCOUNTERED THE concept of theological imagination in my early and mid 20s. I was officially in my progressive Evangelical stage. There was much being awakened in me both academically and ministerially. I was given an introduction to the idea of the Christian imagination and it allowed me to have a new vision of what it might mean to be a Christian in the world, a new world, and one that we had a part to play in creating.

As I have shared thus far, somehow, I have always been ready for the *next*. When I first encountered the idea of using an informed and educated imagination, especially within a hermeneutical framework as we ever endeavor to interpret scripture, I found it so curious and exciting! We could use our imaginations as Christians? Our creativity, ingenuity, and artistry were invited into the process. Also, if something needs to be imagined, then that means it is not yet here, and this was dangerously thrilling.

I started to hear this phrase as it was being referred to within the context of the kingdom of god, *the already and the not yet*. Between my hermeneutics courses and systematic theology classes, learning so much new language and concepts about god, my head was spinning in the best way. My adrenaline was off the charts when class ended. I would be on the phone before I made it back to my car to various friends trying to explain with such wonder and epiphany all that I had just learned. If they didn't answer, I just left them voicemails that eventually cut me off. I guess I was just an evangelist at heart and wanted to share all I was studying and hearing from my professors. While I was a good decade off from learning about radical theology and post-theist thought, I was on the move, as was my theology and as was my imagination.

In some ways, I was poised for it. It played right into my Evangelical eschatology, a new world which was to come. I had developed some sort of theological muscle for it. A precedent was definitely there, but it would be something totally other, and I was ready.

Even as I "coasted," as I spoke about in my first chapter, even when I was too broken to have an imagination for myself, god, and the future, sometimes just taking the next step in the dark, imagining you can take the next step in the dark, is imagination enough.

I spoke early on about Mark C. Taylor's *After God* and how closely I read that book while I was living in the South of France and, even now, return to it often. There was another book I read almost as closely, *Anatheism* by Richard Kearney. Anatheism is the idea of returning to god after God and returning to faith after faith. A lot like, after the death of God, not quite being done with the word god yet.

Part of the question here is with the death of one god, will we have another? Are we Christian Atheists in the sense that we no longer believe in the moral god of our Christian doctrines? What is the way forward for god, faith, and Christianity as we move further into the 21st century, navigating all sorts of realities, stories, landscapes, and contexts? What do we do with our gods and their stories, dead or otherwise? Are there options past normative theism and militant atheism? What is the way forth?

Kearney asks a similar question,

> What comes after God? What follows in the wake of our letting go of God? What emerges out of that night of not-knowing, that moment of abandoning and abandonment? Especially for those who—after ridding themselves of 'God'—still seek God?[2]

These are the questions that most concern and interest me and have also captured the special attention of many who find themselves leaving the church and 'deconstructing.' As I have spoken much on the threat of circles, it seems that metaphor has also been profound for Kearney. He writes of his own journey, "Looking back on my wandering intellectual itinerary, I glimpse it as a set of widening circles."[3] Kearney also understands the peril of the ever-static circle.

Kearney offers an "alternative option of [god's] impossibility."[4] When I was Evangelical, even though I had yet to find language for it, I found myself *spooked* by the notion of impossibility and the impossible god. But I also would think to myself, even though god is deep and wide and, perhaps, unknowable on so many levels, I must believe that god has, is, and will continue to make god's self known to those who seek and search. I think I was halfway there. I stopped at the container, as many do.

Kearney goes past the container and says that "If divinity is unknowable, humanity must imagine it in many ways."[5] Indeed, we must! But we also have to feel the freedom to do so without the parameters of a container that says we can only go so far. The (Un)knowable, as in the event of imagination, not in the being to whom we attribute our imagination.

Early on, Kearney calls hermeneutics to account and rightly so, stating that "Hermeneutics is a lesson in humility."[6] This reminds us that we should approach all things, especially things concerning god, divinity, and the like, with a sense of intellectual, theological, and hermeneutical humility. Too often, this is not the case. When will it be possible for religion to come to the table and say that it is possible we don't know everything, as our knowing is subject to the impossible?

He chooses to use *Other, Stranger,* and *Guest* when referring to god. By using this language, Kearney is attempting to invoke a sense of oneself but also a world that is other. Keeping these two in tandem is key. Anatheism; returning to god after god and "a faith beyond faith [to] serve new life."[7] Ultimately, the question is, how is it that we let go while still seeking at the same time? Kearney offers that there is "another way of seeking and sounding the things we consider sacred but can never fully fathom or prove."[8] He challenges his readers by asking them how exactly they will react when the Stranger appears, with hostility or hospitality.

Kearney pulls from biblical narrative to speak to the event/experience he calls the Stranger or Other. He does his due diligence to pull from all the Abrahamic religions and the Hebrew Scriptures to attest to the fact that Stranger goes beyond being, and he delves into Deuteronomy, as it is rich with references to Stranger. Between Deuteronomy 10, 16, 24, and 27, we see Stranger being depicted in different forms. "First, the stranger is associated with the name of god. Second, the stranger is invariably linked with allusions to orphans and widows...Third, the advent of the stranger calls for a 'justice' that seems to go beyond normal conventions."[9] This is it! An understanding of justice, an arc, and narrative that goes *beyond normal conventions.* One that sets our imaginations soaring, but not to the heights, to the depths. To the outer limits of belief, perhaps we might find a faith worth having and, more importantly, worth living.

Here's the thing, this named Stranger in Kearney's writing. Can we name the Stranger 'god?' Yes. But we must also name the Stranger as orphan, widow, and justice itself. It is *us,* and it is *other.* It is unknowable but strangely recognizable if we can open our imaginations, if we allow the spooking to spook and the ghosts to ghost; if we allow ourselves to become disrupted, infiltrated, and humbled in terms of our notions of god and who we think god is. To even speak of god as 'who' misses the point.

Kearney also calls upon the well-known story of Mary's conception. The young girl visited by a stranger and responds with grace over fear. He uses 'ana' as the point of this story citing "Mary's thinking again, believing again, trusting again."[10] He calls it the first act of Christian Anatheism. He also makes the point that Mary was not "violated" but that she "volunteers." The imagery here is incredible and powerful. So much of Christianity in the West, in particular conservative traditions, operate out of fear and, as a result, end up becoming the aggressor, violating their communities, and sinning against them.

I used to hear often growing up, and in my Evangelical days, *the holy spirit is such a gentleman.* I don't have time here to expand on how harmful using this kind of gendered language, as well as the sexual connotation housed within it, to describe god was and is, so, unfortunately, I need to leave that for now. But the implication of this misused and misappropriated metaphor was that the holy spirit does not and will not force itself upon anyone. It is patient and will wait until that which it is pursuing is ready. So cringe! I'm reminded of the idiom, *the road to hell is paved with good intentions.* The idea here was that God does not *violate* or force encounters but waits upon us to open our hearts. Unfortunately, as much as this idea is peddled, the opposite is actually sold. We are constantly ending up with a violent and violating God that has little regard for us in how this God chooses to intervene or, more than often, not intervene.

This is the dead God. The one whose death we have poured over in earlier chapters. But god after God, post theist, *ana* theist, this is what we volunteer for and to. The Undeconstructible to which we are loyal, that which is worthy of our availability and willingness to wait and wait upon, while all of life waits upon us.

What we see in Western Christianity today and the crisis it finds itself in is the promise and consequence of a particular kind of god construct; the one Nietzsche said was dead, the one Altizer and Hamilton worked to move on from, and the one Mark Taylor says he is living after. Where god is named, contained, and famed as a production of unholy human dreams, the strive for power, prestige, and honor. This is what atheists and so many ex-Christians, and *Exvangelicals*, as well as the *Nones* and *Dones*, are leaving over, raging against, and 'deconstructing' from. Kearney's Anatheism is one example of new ways to engage theologically, narratively, linguistically, and even biblically. This is rediscovering the sacred, should we choose to call it such, every day, again and again; *ana*.

A faith after faith is what Kearney and others are after. While it isn't perfect or exhaustively conclusive, we know that we are headed in a more human direction (not to be confused with a more *humanist* direction). One that defies categories or rather transcends them, one that recognizes what we know in terms of the unknowing and one that allows faith to return to us as a stranger and guest and, more importantly, other, as we greet it with radical hospitality and continue in our spiral never to be the same again.

This is imagination. This is theological imagination. It is a post-Christian imagination.

GOD, FAITH, THE IMPOSSIBLE, AND THE LANGUAGE GAME WE MUST PLAY

Language is extremely important in this discussion. As John Caputo once wrote, "if we want to change theology—or anything else—change the metaphors."[11] We don't often realize the weight that words hold, what they house, and what they theologize all on their own. And while most of us will never be full-time philosophers, we have to hold all our language so loosely, even the new language and the new language when that language becomes old. It is all an attempt. It is an experiment with crystallizing event. It is an endeavor to make faith possible, by which we are in danger of it no longer being *faith*.

So, what are we to do? It is quite a maddening conundrum. If it feels this way to you, you might be on your way to understanding it all. If it vexes you or troubles you, or even feels like a fool's errand, keep going. You are starting upon an unfixed and unknown path that is *safer than the known way*.

In an interview with Mark Dooley, Jacques Derrida was asked about the "undecidable fluctuation between the passion for '*the* impossible' and the passion for God."[12] Dooley asked Derrida to respond to what seemed to be an unsolvable riddle put forth by his greatest theological proponent and colleague. Derrida said that the difference was "the name."[13] This is not the difference between the Impossible and God, but rather the passion for each. But here is when we return to Alice's looking glass as a guest at the Mad Hatter's tea party. Derrida goes on to say,

"The impossible" is not a name, it is not a proper name, it is not some*one*. "God"—I do not say divinity—is someone with a name, even if it is a nameless name like the Jewish god. It is a nameable nameless name, whereas *the* impossible is a non-name, a common name, a non-proper name. "God" is a proper nameable nameless name. "*The* impossible" is a common non-proper name, or nameless common name. Now, you cannot and you should not translate one into the other. If there is a transparent translatability "the faith" is safe, that is, it becomes a non-faith. At that point, it becomes possible to name. It becomes possible because there is some*one* whom you can name and call because you know who it is that you are calling. Not only can I not say this, but I would not and should not say this. If I were sure that it was possible for me to replace "*the* impossible" by "God, " then everything would become possible. Faith would become possible, and when faith becomes simply possible it is not faith anymore. So I see a danger for faith and for something which is the abyss of faith. This danger consists in stating, or in believing in, the mere translatability between the two things.[14]

After reading sentiments like these, one might see why he had so many critics and those in his field who simply brushed him off. Because at first glance, it follows a *here not there, there not here* rhythm. Suppose ood enough to chalk up the naming of the Impossible as God due to language frailty and insufficiency. In that case, faith is completely negated and is no longer possible precisely because we have made it possible. Faith is an abyss; it is *the* abyss. We can surrender ourselves to its unknowable, Impossible, and what seems like beyond-imagination-movements, fully aware of the incognizance of it all, or we can call it God. But we cannot do both.

The former is what the post-Christian conversation is all about, the latter is something you might read about in some progressive Christian book looking for the low-hanging fruit. "God" is reductionistic, and perhaps the Impossible is god with a difference. But the difference is the change in track, which alters the destination completely, leaving us without one. Take the risk if you dare; continuing on in faithfulness to the non-faith which compels us to be faithless with an imagination informed only by the wonder of our very breath.

Yet, in the spirit of not subscribing to a this or that understanding of what may be represented within linguistic tokens and what may not be, let me include this helpful note from Caputo on the otherness of god and language,

> The other is never simply inside or outside language. The other is never conceivable or referable except by means of the resources of linguistic difference, yet it is never reducible to a string of signifiers. The other is a being of marginality, on the margins of language, occupying the point of contact where language opens up to things and where things break in upon and break open language.[15]

mysticism.

It is a matter of rendering language obsolete. Because perhaps the Impossible is beyond language and beyond non-language. It happens in real-time at the margins of it all. Enough so we can feel the propensity of its gusts and currents without knowing where it came from or where it is going, but faithfully living in the light of its consecrated return, as long as you are alive, as long as you are human, all of life exists at the intersectionality of unspeakable things that are only transmuted in the world by the living of them.

One thing to remember is that deconstruction has not "appointed itself the supreme arbiter of what is true and false. On the contrary, it is because it confesses that it does not 'know' the 'secret' that sits in the middle and smiles at our ignorance."[16] Deconstruction does not reduce "the world to words without references." Rather it asks us to think the unthinkable, past binaries, listening as best we can to the whispers that communicate the ineffable, the shocking and unbelievable audacity of the fullness of faithfulness to *That* which we have faith in and that which we challenge with all our absurd imagination and a wicked spark of vision.

THE PERILS OF THE KNOWN IMAGINATION

Sometimes, when we expand our imaginations, we don't go quite far enough. We no longer believe what we once did, and so we move towards a belief that allows us to think bigger thoughts. Thoughts that make more sense and can put into perspective all that we can account for and all that we can't. However, the only thing it seemingly accounts for is our addiction to certainty, our need to know, and our love affair with naming, claiming, and subsequently containing.

nailed down vs under construction

I have alluded to this earlier in chapter five, and I would be amiss if I didn't talk about what we can sometimes use as substitutions as far as language is concerned as we move on from the constraints of the word *god*. I want to try and be clear, although clear is not this book's strong suit. I am not condemning or ostracizing, I am interrogating and asking us to be honest about what is taking place in the name of the language we use.

The whole world watched as we received the beautiful, mind-boggling images from the James Webb Space Telescope. They were literally otherworldly. We were able to have a small window into galaxies that existed 4.6 billion years ago. They are incredible images to behold. Lights and flames and dust and stars, hydrocarbons and chemical compounds that not only existed in glorious technicolor billions of years ago, but it has been reported by NASA that if you were to hold a grain of sand at arm's length this would be the measurement of space we are looking at. This is utterly sensational, and it simply ravishes our day-to-day lives with not only beauty but the thought we are just a small speck of all that has been and ever will be.

Over the last few to several years, a trend has resurfaced, appropriating words like 'Universe' and exchanging them for problematic theological rhetoric like 'God.' Most would say the word and concept of 'God' is limiting and because so many still see themselves as inherently spiritual, they aren't willing to give up a Divine Other; a force and agency in the world that perhaps looks out for us, allows us to manifest our best lives, and flows blessings into our existence. Our life is good. We find beauty and joy in it all. And we need something to make it all make sense. So, there has been a move from the word 'God' to the word 'Universe.'

I use the term 'resurfaced' because this is nothing new. It is an adaptation and a position that has cyclically come around again and again. However, it has now been re-popularized among progressive and post Evangelicals, in a move that feels liberating to a new generation of believers and/or ex-believers. Still, it is deceptively homogenous and akin to the big God in the sky.

I, too, am in awe of the universe. I am bewitched by quantum physics and besotted by the processes of creation and re-creation in our world and galaxies. I, too, have been caught up in the beautiful spin of what feels like magic and the incredible and unpredictable alchemy of life. But I'm uninterested in allowing my imagination to be so small and pre programmed as to simply transact the noun of god for the noun of universe.

To be fair, it is hard to leave the big God in the sky behind, and most of us do because we are left with no choice after being presented repeatedly with zero viability for such a god. So, it is an easy transition and quite a bit more palatable to employ the language of universe to try and fill that big gaping hole we will sometimes feel in our identities. This assures us that there is still a grand purpose, and something somewhere might still have our back and our best interests at heart.

I would never begrudge anyone their process or their journey. However, I would caution against making this little more than a pit stop on your 'deconstruction' journey. Because this isn't deconstruction, it is just having a bit of a go at a bigger big G God.

I have seen people engage with the Universe as they have engaged with their former God(s); act a certain way, and there will be a return on your investment. Speak certain words because Someone or Something is listening and will reward you. Follow the rules, and it will all work out for you. Worship the Universe and live by its creed, and all will be well. This is a dangerous place to be and a perilous ideology to possess. And it is anything but new and anything but progressive.

There is still a faith in a particular kind of certainty required to be in play here, and I'm worried that it is nothing more than the other side of the same coin. We once described our God as omniscient, omnipotent, and omnipresent. Now we describe the Universe as such and call it radical. It isn't radical. Not at all. But it is safe, it is *safe* because it *is the known way*. There is no shame or blame in that, as long as we know what it is we are doing and we are honest with ourselves about that.

We use religious and propositional language to speak of the Universe, and we aren't always aware that we are doing so. When we are unaware of this, then we are under the illusion that we are free when we are not. We have simply decided to worship God by a different name, continuing to enslave ourselves to certainty.

Gordon Kaufman, in his book, *In the beginning...Creativity*, writes,

> What, then, are we to make of the paraphrase of the opening words of the Fourth Gospel with which this chapter began: "In the beginning was creativity, and... [this] creativity was God"? Two quite different interpretations come to mind. In the ordinary understanding of John's Gospel, it is usually assumed that to say "the Word was God" (1:1) is a declaration that the Word (which a few verses later will be identified with Jesus) is fully divine. John goes on to emphasize this point immediately by stating, "All things came into being through" this Word (1:3); this is what created the heavens and the earth.

Were we to follow this pattern of interpretation, my paraphrase would be redundant, simply asserting that the
"creativity" that brought all things into being is nothing
other than the activity of the creator—and we would be
left with our familiar ideas about both God and creativity. The other interpretations of the paraphrase, however,
turns this all around and asserts that the phrase "creativity
was [or is] God: is not redundant at all but rather a claim
about what our word "God" designates; it is *creativity*
that is God; when we use the word "God" it is the profound mystery of creativity to which we are referring,
and it would be a mistake, therefore, to let the familiarity
of our personalistic images and ideas of God get in the
way of our recognizing the significance of this point. The
word "creativity," as we have been noting, leaves the question of how or why the new comes into being completely
open, and (in this second interpretation) the word "God"
is the religious name for this mystery that goes beyond
human understanding. This interpretation implies that
we should beware of unconsciously importing any images or idea—personalistic or other—into our thinking
about God, for that would be refusing to acknowledge
the ultimacy of God's (creativity's) profound mystery,
instead of facing up to what that mystery means for us.
It would be claiming we know something that we cannot
possibly know, why and how there is something and not
nothing.[17]

If we need new language, we must do our best to choose a metaphor that gets as close as we can to the wild vastness and undomesticated nature of whatever it is we are trying to speak about. It is not about what or who the newness flows through, to be dispensed to us mere mortals, but rather it is the fact that it flows at all. Kaufman calls this 'creativity.' Derrida called it 'event.' Caputo has called it 'spectral.' But whatever it is, it is nothing established and nothing understood. And 'creativity' isn't even the best we can do. Our concepts, thoughts, and humanity are all moving faster than our language can possibly keep up. But whatever it is we are trying to speak of, describe, name, reference, and bear witness to, one thing is for sure. While there is, indeed, a profound mystery, the question isn't what or who we attribute this mystery to, but, ultimately, what does this mystery mean for us here and now? Without giving name and acclaim to it in the way that feels most natural, or rather most tempting, where might our imaginations lead us as it subverts the sky god towards an integral journey that is *safer than the known way*.

WHY THE CHRISTIAN IN POST-CHRISTIAN

"What comes after the Post Age? What might a post-Post Age be?"[1]

— Mark C. Taylor

THE *POST* IN POST-CHRISTIAN

LANGUAGE CAN'T POSSIBLY KEEP up with the ever-changing flow of thoughts, culture, narratives, philosophies, and experience—the life force spinning around us. One can think about artificial intelligence in the post-human movement. One can speak about new ways of thinking past mere critical interaction and call post-critical. There has been much talk about post-liberal ideology. Things are moving too fast to be named, it seems. All we know is that it isn't what it once was. Not in a way that is opposite, but different. It is not the antithesis of where it came from but is completely past it, rendering it obsolete. Obsolete because usually, it is answering a question no one is asking. In the wake of new thought, we call it *post*. We do this partly because what has arrived would not have come to us had it not been on the heels of the thing it finds itself past; post.

Carl Raschke has this to say about the *post* in postmodernism, it "marks little more than the disruption of, or transition beyond, what has gone before."[2] Mark Taylor talks about it in terms of "post ages." In a nod to Soren Kierkegaard, he writes that it is easy for philosophy to begin but difficult for it to end. "Uncertain of what comes next, the series becomes a series, perhaps an infinite series of post ages...What comes after the Post Age? What might a post-Post Age be?"[3] We can't characterize or name an age until it is almost over. So, this leaves us with the ambiguous, imprecise, nebulous expression, *post*.

Not only are we unable to name what comes next, but we also do not know what is to come next. We just know what we are beyond. Yet it has not ended. It has simply run its course, and is now evolving into something different, standing on the shoulders of its legacy, both good and bad. We know what we don't want, but do we know what we want? If we are no longer looking for absolute certainty, can we name the uncertainty we desire?

People have called me many things when I have used the term, post-Christian. Atheist, Christian atheist, agnostic, backslider, unbeliever, unorthodox, and heretic. Sometimes I have been subjected to various religious rhetoric inferring that I've strayed. However, to accept any of these classifications I would have to be something other than what has come after my Christianity. I am unapologetically and indefensibly not that. I am all and everything that has come after my Christianity. I am all that has come after a personal relationship with the sky God, his son, and his spirit. I am all that has come after years of prayer, bible study, charismatic and pentecostal expressions of spirituality, evangelism, and the like. I am all that has come after the curious girl staring up into cathedrals domes that wondered what was beyond it all. This is all I am.

I'll never forget hearing the phrase 'post' for the first time in a religious context. I had just started work in administration for a liberal seminary after coming from an Evangelical one. The liberal seminary, like most seminaries, found itself with decreasing enrollment and funds and was working to reinvent itself into an institution that would be useful and effective for preparing ministers for the work of the 21st-century church. The more conservative seminary I had left, while it had flourished for a few years as it grew more progressive, decided to re-entrench itself in its former conservative and fundamental values, thinking this might be the answer to their enrollment woes.

At my new seminary, we started to use the term post-Evangelical to describe our ideal students. We were not looking to stay siloed in liberal vs. conservative seminary. We wanted to be "post" both of those. We wanted to be attractive to Evangelicals who were moving on but would feel out of place in liberal Protestant faith environments. We also wanted to capture the attention of liberal Protestants who detested conservative religious values. Somehow the word post-Evangelical captured the right sentiment.

The first known use of this phrase was by British vicar and writer Dave Tomlinson in his 1995 book, *The Post-Evangelical*. In 1995, I was 13 years old and had no idea that what I believed had a name other than

Christianity. The way I understood it, one was either Catholic or they were what I was becoming, which in those early days of my newfound faith among a sea of New York Roman Catholics was *born-again*. I had no cognizance of Evangelicalism and certainly not post-Evangelicalism.

Tomlinson tells a story of attempting to regain the original aims of Evangelicalism in Britain as opposed to the rigid, graceless, dogmatic, toxic system it had become. This familiar idea of those who wanted Jesus, not the church and those who sought freedom of faith instead of manufactured ideology. Not only was it radical, but it also created a community and camaraderie that allowed many wayward ex-Evangelicals to feel less alone. In the reprinting of his book 19 years after its original publish date, he says this in his new preface,

> But none of this is simply about a problem within evangelicalism. A similar story has been unfolding in other traditions. Sometimes people contact me saying they are 'post-Catholic', 'post-liberal' and various other 'posts'. This is not surprising because the underlying issue is about the relationship between faith and culture, which affects all religious traditions. The ideas that the substance of our faith can remain precisely the same regardless of significant changes taking place all around is completely mistaken. The journey of faith always raises a conversation between inherited beliefs and contemporary sensibilities.[4]

Therein lies the rub.. Most Evangelical and fundamental Christians believe faith is immovable, or to use their vernacular, *unshakable*.

On Christ the solid rock I stand,

All other ground is sinking sand.

That is how the popular hymn goes. It invokes a nostalgia strong enough to sustain a sense of righteous indignation that refuses conversation. Martyr complexes set in, and suddenly, they are fighting for the uncompromising nature of their God and faith. I wish it weren't so, but in my work, the groups I talk with the least are those given to a specific, unmistakable heralding of Christianity. It is because they simply do not want to have a conversation that, for them, wreaks of blasphemy and someone who has lost their way unto their fleshly desires. I do my best not to create talking points based on 'us' and 'them' rhetoric. But sometimes, it just can't be helped.

The truth is (as if we are not post-truth in some senses) nothing is unshakable or immovable. Certainly not while event and l'avenir are dancing around us. As the world turns, and humanity changes how it responds to such turns, the needs of those seeking spiritual engagement, peace, meaning-making, and, of course, God, the sacred, and the divine must also change. I think Tomlinson got it right when discussing the tension between "inherited beliefs and contemporary sensibilities." This tension is why faith and Christianity, and certainly God, are in crisis and continue to be.

"Inherited beliefs" beg us to compromise our sense of intellect, reason, experience, intuition, and imagination. The pressure is too much at some point, leaving us in rubble and ruin, and a massive identity crisis. It leaves us with the painfully already answered question of 'what is next' but not in the form of post-Christianity. In a way that has left us destitute. And the question has become rhetorical, as we feel the bitter sting of loss, nothingness, and an unholy introduction to the abyss that seems to be staring us right in the face.

Facing this abyss is where we become *post*. Post all we are standing in, which is now dust and rubble. With a biblical imagination that tells us we were once dust and to dust we shall return. But where will the dust lead us now? The wind of l'avenir blows, kicking up a cloud of ash. It forms a ghost, and it speaks. Perhaps it sighs, 'fear not.' This ghost is the *post* of post-Christian. This ghost is the teasing and taunting of all the future, and indeed the present may become if we choose imagination over nostalgia.

THE *CHRISTIAN* IN POST-CHRISTIAN

This past summer, while visiting friends in Paris, my husband and I toured various villages and cities in northern France. One such city was Amiens. It was glorious, as so much of France is. Wherever we are, Simon and I always look out for bookstores. The more independent, used, secondhand and rare, the better! There was a shop that didn't look like a shop, a few minutes from the city center. The owner of the shop was an older gentleman with white hair and a swoon-worthy, French-accented English. I am always in awe and grateful for the graciousness and hospitality of the French, and their willingness to speak English. My French is bad, despite the amount of time I have spent in France. In the time it takes me to get a heavily accented, clumsy sentence out slowly, they are well on their way to assuring me it's easier to speak English. This old man was one such Frenchman.

Several books were strewn in old, broken down boxes, lining the outside of the shop. During my search, I found a box marked 2€. As I peered inside, I could see they were theological books. Almost a complete set of musty, leather-bound volumes of *Vies Des Saints*. I carefully picked each one up and stowed them under my arms, up to my elbows, and in my hands. I picked up yet another 19th-century, leather-bound book. Written in gold on the binding, *Compendium Theologiae Moralis*. And another, *L'imitation De Esus-Christ*. I was running out of hands, so I put them all back in the box, and bought them all. The beautiful older Frenchman explained there were more inside, and I should have a look, which, of course, I did.

There were no bookshelves. There were just a few rooms, one leading into the other. Tables lined the edges along with countless brown boxes. The old man had stacked dozens of art pieces against each other, and old drawings in piles. I was a kid in a candy shop. I tried to explain what I was looking for–Christian books. Old ones like those in the box.

I came across a tiny book of similar age and binding: *La Vie Dévote*. A small book of 600 pages filled with prayers and devotional practices, all in French, from a time gone by. How could I possibly leave this beautiful little find behind? So, I bought it. I can see it now from where I write. I've translated the first line of the preface, "please read this preface for your benefit and mine." What a clever little line. What benefit is it to the author that the reader reads the preface? Yet it makes sense. The author wants you to be informed before you start. To lay a foundation; almost a subtext, the energy and force with which the author wants you to read with intention.

This phrase, *la vie dévote*, a devoted life, haunted me. Our Airbnb in Amiens was at the top of a five-floor building. My husband chose it because the writing desk had the most breathtaking view of Notre-Dame d'Amiens. He knew I would love it. Each day I sat looking out my window with a clear symbol of devotion. I also now had this small reader with its gold-inscripted title. And, perhaps, the biggest token of all, I had myself, which is no less than a life devoted.

Some might ask what my life is devoted to. Outside of the usual answers that one may be tempted to give: family, friends, work, etc., what does it mean for someone like me, who claims to be post-God, to have a *devoted life*? Clearly, this is a religious devotional for those following the orthodox bounds of the long-standing traditions of Western Christianity. So how might I be attaching myself to it? While I feel I would qualify as someone who could identify their existence with this little phrase (in English and/or in French), I had to take some time to think long and hard about why I wanted to claim these small language units for myself. I think by virtue of being post-Christian is reason enough. I haven't left Christianity, I have simply diverted my gaze in a different direction. Perhaps it would be more of an adjustment of orientation. The shifting landscape and altering horizon have reoriented me in a new direction. Is it true to say I have left some things behind? Sure. But it is more that I have finished with them, and, to be fair, they have finished with me. I haven't moved on unto nothing or even Something, but the (un)determined next point on a map that is provided only after you fall off the first one.

Again, an invitation to the Mad Hatter's tea party. Because I understand how crazy and even nonsensical it might sound. But this is the essence of the journey. To take the risks that seem to most unreasonable, with a gripping, confident, and scary faith that there is something better. Even if the better is nothingness, we are no longer trapped in confines that couldn't hold us and were so painful when they tried.

I have found psychoanalysis illuminating, helpful, and nurturing to my humanity and religious healing. While I have not referenced it, I have to make note of psychoanalyst Mari Ruth's work, and her book, *A World of Fragile Things: Psychoanalysis and the Art of Living.*

> WE LIVE IN a world of fragile things: fragile selves, fragile psyches, fragile loves. One of the most distinctive features of human existence—what makes it recognisable as human and what gives it its characteristically bittersweet quality—is that we tend to be acutely aware of this precariousness even when we are more or less courageously focused on taking advantage of the various opportunities that it affords. Human life is therefore inherently paradoxical in the sense that we strive to make the most of circumstances that we know will end disastrously, with our own death. As Schopenhauer once put it, we insist on living our lives "with great interests and much solicitude as long as possible, just as we blow out a soap-bubble as long and as large as possible, although with the perfect certainty that it will burst."[5]

This way of thinking is meaningful on many levels. It is almost always helpful to remember that our lives are short and precarious. Even in the moments of excitement, where we blow the bubble big and wide, feeling like it will never end, yet it will end. With 100% certainty, the bubble will pop, and it will be over. In this sense, it is a paradox to live our human lives, as we are driven to make the most of it while knowing that it will, in fact, end. And, with a few generations, no one will even remember we were alive. The push and pull of the meaningful and meaningless. This is what it means to be human. And, if I can be so bold, this is what it means to be post-Christian.

Christianity promises an escape from meaninglessness and an escape from death. The billing reads we no longer have to live in the paradox that some might name as sin because we have indeed been rescued from it. How easy to live a life devoted to this particular narrative, as it promises so much. Unfortunately, too much. And these promises can't hold. They pop as all bubbles do.

But when we hop the track, get out of this narrative loop, broken record, and truly fantastical ideation, we find a life we must live on life's terms. It is up to us how we want to engage meaning and push past the existential dread of impending death. When we live undeterred by this and *live*(!) anyway, this is a life devoted.

Life is fragile. Our stories hold us. All we have been through, our communities, our relationships, and our experiences. But it will all come to an end. Yet when we realize the fragility of it all, knowing it could end at any moment, and live right in the face of it, we live a life devoted. Devoted to all that our life, no matter how brief or unknown, might have for us. Devoted to our stories and the continual writing of them. Devoted to all parts of ourselves as we continue to become. Devoted to moving on from all we might have once been devoted to, for the sake of falling off that map to possibly encounter all that might be next.

I am devoted to my past and to the God I once knew in the sense that I am true to the trajectory of my Chris where it has taken me, and where it will continue to go. And precisely because of my devotion to my story and my own (de)conversion, I get to keep my story. I don't have to check my entire spiritual narrative at the door. I don't have to give up how I decide to involve myself with Jesus of the gospels. I don't have to walk away from scripture because of hermeneutical perplexities and complexities. I don't have to say it was all for nothing, it doesn't matter. It deeply matters, and I get to live my life in light of it all.

Post-Christian doesn't have to mean post-Jesus, post-faith, and it certainly doesn't have to mean that those things are *post* being important to us! It does mean that we frame it all a little differently, as evidenced by what you have read thus far. Our currency is not empirical but theological. We aren't so much concerned with realities of being, transcendence, supernaturalism, historicity, or even facticity. Rather we want the transformation that comes with a living story, one that is interpreted as it is lived and written as it is disrupted and interrupted.

So, why shouldn't we speak of Christianity, Jesus, and ever seek ways to engage it all, what it was, what it is and is not, a little better? What does it look like to be faithful as a post-Christian? Is there such a thing? Is it possible? Is it even desirable?

Earlier in my chapter on "Jesus After Saviorism", I said that sometimes in more liberal or progressive forms of Christianity, it can be difficult to differentiate Jesus from a humanitarian. Because there has been so much division around Christology that we would rather not choose a side, divine or human or both and how much of each. But as post-Christians, we must ask ourselves about the difference

Jesus might make in all of this. What is the Christian distinctive in *post-Christian* and what makes it so?

In Carter Heyward's *Saving Jesus from Those Who Are Right: Rethinking What It Means to Be Christian*, she writes,

> Christians are called more than anything to be faithful, not "right.".…Through his teachings, healing, and prophetic resistance to state-sponsored and religious-based legalism that disregarded human need, Jesus reflected the incarnate (embodied) Spirit of One who was not then, and is not ever, contained solely in one human life or religion or historical event or moment. God was Jesus' relational power, more specifically his power for forging right (mutual) relation in which Jesus himself and those around him were empowered to be more fully who they were called to be. We today are also empowered by this same mutual relation.[6]

Heyward speaks about being faithful to the example of mutual relation and relationship given to us by One, the spirit of One, the god of One, aka the dream of unity and community. But she also goes on to say,

> I assume that Jesus actually lived; that he was a man about whom we know little, probably less than we think do, certainly less than a literal reading of the biblical record would suggest. At the same time, I recognize that Jesus is

a figure of mythic (symbolic) proportions about whom we may know a great deal more than we often imagine we can, more than the Bible actually can tell us.[7]

So we are called to be faithful, indeed. Devoted, one might say. But perhaps the literal life of Jesus barely comes into it. Is that possible? Is it possible to be "faithful," as Heyward calls it, without espousing to savior-of-the-world motifs, spun into existence by the self-absorbed way of the West? Yes, I know. A leading question to say the least. But this is my point. Just because we don't engage Jesus like most of Christendom has done for 1700 years doesn't mean we don't get to interact with the work, narrative, and even spirit of Christ. Spirit in the sense of specter, character, and courage.

Perhaps, the most important work of all is the task of unification, in the sense of mutuality, respect, hospitality, love, and caring for the other. These are humanitarian values to be sure, but more than this, that which makes it distinctly Christic is the role Jesus plays in this task for us. We will never know with certainty the person of Jesus, the historical Jesus, the Jesus of the Bible, or the Jesus of tradition. Jesus' story has been told and retold. It has shaped Western culture, been co-opted, incorporated, and converted to Western values of power, prestige, mastery, and muscle. It has been owned and dominated by all those who believe they are "right." But maybe we can encounter this work of mutuality as we call forth the best in each other. How is this Christic? Well maybe, as Heyward writes...

> Rather than embodying, all by himself, the power of
> God, he was someone through whose presence and with
> whom friends and strangers began to notice the power of
> God stirring among them, with them all, perhaps actually
> "in" them from moment to moment. From this perspec-
> tive, Jesus was not the exception, he was the norm—the
> normal human being, what each of us is created to be.[8]

Heyward uses the word "normal" and I would agree-normal and *fully human*. Living as we were created and intended. To be in the right relationship with each other, ourselves, and our world. And what if our lives reflected this ethos?

We don't have to decide if Jesus was the Son of God or simply a moral teacher. If he was a prophet or a political prisoner. We just have to recognize the life he called others to. A life of fullness of community, relationality, mutuality, and humanity. This creed and Christology are more than good enough for me, and it makes the task of *Christian* in post-Christian worth the price of admission.

8

"HE IS NOT HERE..."

"And if anyone says to you at that time, 'Look! Here is the Messiah' or 'Look! There he is!'—do not believe it."

— Mark 13:21

"But he said to them, "Do not be alarmed; you are looking for Jesus of Nazareth, who was crucified. He has been raised; he is not here."

— Mark 16:6

DEATH OF A SAVIOR

UNDER THE SECTION TITLED *"The inconsolable departure,"* Martin Heidegger writes, "The twisting free is not consolation in the sense of a dissolving of the pain but, instead, requires redemption in the pain of questioning that which is question-worthy."[1] The process I have done my best to describe, has not been without pain. It is not without its deep sense of loss and mind-dizzying grief. The noble task of asking questions of "that which is question-worthy" is, sometimes, our only guiding light. That the task is worthy and that we are, indeed, up for the task.

As I mentioned in chapter two, from time to time, in the presence of friends and colleagues, I will sometimes hear that they miss the "always-there-and-ready-with-an-answer-savior." They miss the solace of knowing Someone was looking after them and watching out for them. Even if they were all alone in the world, there was a presence that brought peace and calm in raging and chaotic storms. I can only listen on with sympathy and a sense of pastoral care that I feel so often as I do this work. Because the loss is so real, my heart goes out to them and bleeds for them.

While I have had various grief stages throughout my faith transition(s), and I say this with zero hubris and more with dumbfounded astonishment, I have never felt compelled to miss what I once knew, enjoyed, and possessed. This is surprising to me. And I have done my best to search myself on this. Am I not being honest with myself? Have I somehow hardened to the pain of it all? Am I avoiding the ache? I have asked myself these questions because I really want to know. The truth is I can remember feeling desperately alone. I can remember feeling like there was no one I could talk to and no life raft in a roaring sea. I can remember feeling shame at not knowing and feeling like I was in great danger of irreparably losing my way. But I never felt an anger toward God or like I wanted to shake my fist to the sky and offer up choice words. I never felt like I had debunked Jesus and was now free to step on and over his legacy and move on. I just had a profound and abiding feeling that my orientation to it all was changing.

I didn't want to rush whatever was happening. I also didn't want to talk to a bunch of people about it either because the last thing I needed was tons of unnecessary and unhelpful opinions clouding my brain. I just wanted to be. Alone. Watching the tumbleweeds blow by. But even in this aloneness, I never wished for the savior I once knew. And I have never been one for numbing or dulling my senses just to make it through. I have always valued honesty and straight talk. However, I haven't always been the best at it due to years of people pleasing, which was a maladaptive coping mechanism to environments of trauma at a formative age.

My very first time in the office of a therapist was in my early 20s. I had to attend one session to talk over the results of a personality assessment I had to do for seminary. I don't remember much from that hour except one line that will stay with me for the rest of my life. I was told I had an incredibly high tolerance for pain. I have been told the same by doctors, in particular a chiropractor and physical therapist. Apparently, both emotionally and physically, I have the capacity to endure a lot. I don't think this is something to boast of. I'm not sure it is a healthy trait, nor did it develop in a healthy environment, but here we are. So maybe there was a bit of built-in, automatic pilot, self-preservation happening. But also, maybe I just knew my God was no longer there, and somehow that was ok.

I have always been perplexed by the reaction of the disciples to Jesus' disappearance from the tomb in John's gospel. Mary Magdalene goes to the tomb, as is reported in other gospels. She can see the stone has been moved. So she goes to the disciples explaining that Jesus is not there. She is bereft and in inconsolable anguish. All we know is that the next thing that happens is "Peter and the other disciple" (20:3) are on their way towards the tomb. The other disciple runs in to see Jesus' burial clothes just lying there. Peter came in and beheld the same. They looked for Jesus where he should be, and he was not there. But then we read that "the disciples simply returned to their homes" (20:10). You gave *one* look. You went on *one* search. You expected Jesus to be in the tomb, but when you looked, he wasn't there, so you just left and went home. Mary stayed and cried. She simply sat there and wept. She wasn't thinking of the task of finding him. She didn't hunt around the garden or anywhere else. She knew he wasn't there, and she wept.

I find this little narrative quite profound. It is permeated with a keen sense of devotion to that which we know not where it is. We just know it is not here. So many times in my life, I was like the disciples, looking for God, for this Jesus I knew, to be exactly where I left him, to be explicitly where he was expected to be, where I knew he would be, and where he had been before. But I have come to know that which we call 'god' is never where it is to be expected. At some point, I found myself in the shoes of Mary. Plainly seeing he isn't there, weeping, knowing there was nothing to be done about it. And then the unexpected happens, a plot twist of poetic proportions.

Jesus appears to Mary, and she supposes him to be the gardener, tending to the terrace where the dead God had been laid to rest. A gardener that would cultivate life out of death, and duration and survival out of such damage and decay. Attending to the composting of what once lived, that is now dead but will enrich all that is to come. Perhaps that is all going a bit too far with the gardener metaphor, but what a fabulous mistake for her to make.

In response to her realizing that it is, in fact, Jesus, he urges, "Do not hold on to me" (20:17). Brilliant. Done. *Do not look for me here, and if you should find me in an unexpected moment, then still, do not hold on to me.*

This is how I felt. This is what gave me peace through the pain. Holding on would have been the *known way*, but I was about to travel *safer than the known way* because the task of questioning the "question-worthy" was to be all the redemption I would need if redemption was, in fact, the curious concern.

When Raschke talks about the significance of Derrida's deconstruction, he says, "deconstruction of texts shows us what is signified is never immediate to us. On the contrary, when we go back to find it, we discover that it has evaporated. As Derrida puts it, the only true paradise is lost paradise."[2] Whatever we are looking for is gone, and it was gone the moment it took form. The present is never something that is afforded to us. We are only ever remembering a past just gone or about to live the future. The present is a vapor, and what we have collected as present realities are evaporated fumes of what just was. Now I know we don't live our lives this way, and why would we? Some would say that this is just highfalutin philosophical mumbo jumbo. But I urge us to be challenged with these concepts because perhaps it will inspire us to realize our fearfully tight grip on all that we think we know.

Being that deconstruction, as used and expounded upon by Derrida, was and is first applied to literature, Raschke sums it up like this, "Writing erases the meaning of what once was written."[3] The idea here is that the moment we encapsulate anything in any container, signifier, name, and nomenclature, we have already started to subject it to erasure, *"sous rature."*[4]

"When we go back to find it..."

The disciples went back to find something. The disciples found nothing, nor were they interested in looking in unexpected places. They didn't even wait; to stop for a moment in their grief. Mary also went back to find something. She also did not recover what she was initially searching for. But as she waited and cried, she caught a glimpse of something different, and even though she responded to it as she thought she should, it was gone again. But not before it filled her with the hope of the unknown, the anticipation of all that might come, and a fresh imagination for what she was searching for.

He is not here...

A WORD ON KINGDOMS

This entire book has been about what exactly is going on in the name of god? What occurs within this infamous noun that has been many things to many people, but has usually always meant strong, powerful, mighty, glorious being? Caputo says that the force of event is "sheltered by the name of God."[5] But he says it is a weak force, a "powerless power," that we can choose to "ignore—at our peril."[6] It isn't a power with a show of strength and no reinforcements can aid or assist. It does not demand or drag but will disrupt and dislodge all we thought we were holding together.

Traditionally when we have spoken about the kingdom of God, we have done so with a backdrop of ultimate victory. The unseen kingdom that we pray will overlap with the world and in the age to come, will overthrow and reign for eternity. God is king, and we are forever worshiping subjects. Caputo says, "In the New Testament, the event goes under the name 'kingdom of God'...filled in or fleshed out...in soaring parables and mind-bending paradoxes."[7] We see the "weak force" of event spoken of in the upside-down parables in which all earthly and kingdomly values are turned on their heads. The parables whisper of a kingdom that is unknown to us, a kingdom for which there is no precedent and is beyond compare. He says this is the kingdom that we respond with, "'May your kingdom come,' *viens, oui, oui.*"[8]

We cannot escape the fact that religion has had a love affair with power. Even those who speak of the weak and meek, the humble and the hermits, believe that God is the ultimate vindicator and that all power shall bow to that which will be the power to end all powers. They follow a military king of the cosmos that is lying in wait for the right now, and they lie with them. Their followers claim to live in subversion to the world, but they couldn't be in more accord with its obsession with dominance, sovereignty, and control. They've ignored the whispers, they seek to stop at 'God' rather than smash through it to find what is behind and beyond.

Caputo likens the kingdom of God to anarchy, "a sacred anarchy."[9] He takes this all a step further and says that rather than *'arche'* it is *'anarche.'*[10]

Is it possible that we are to think of the kingdom of God a-arche, without arc? Or even ana-arche, after arc? Without a polished, neat, predictable story arc, the kind of arc we can see on the horizon, and we know exactly where it ends and where it starts. To be beyond arc, transcending the arc, diverting the storyline unto where one does not know, which is precisely why we do so. In this sense, we are not anarchists in the kingdom of God, the kingdom of god is itself anarchy, but a "sacred anarchy." It is not simply the opposite of held and established values, it confounds all that might make sense. If we were to think of it as an antithesis, there would still be a level of reasonable understanding because opposites we know and recognize. It is other, and this is indefinable. It is the opposite plus or minus an undiscovered sum.

It is that which we can say nothing other than *viens, oui, oui,* come, yes, yes.

The kingdom of the Impossible. Rather than a God by which all is possible, we have the event of god by which it is all impossible. Somehow the coming of l'avenir reaches back and reaches forward, it touches with a skimming graze the possible, and infuses it with the Impossible, leaving behind ghostly embers which are barely discernible as having any illumination at all, so much so you may only see darkness. Unless, perhaps, our imaginations have been readied and steadied, and we are lucky enough to catch the wink of the wicked little bit of quivering and shivering radiance.

9

OUR LITTLE MESS AND DUST EVERYWHERE

"Life is immanently what it is: Always different from
itself while never separating itself from itself. Such is the
meaning of plasticity."[1]

— **Catherine Malabou**

THE CHALLENGE OF THE DUST

THE WORK AND JOURNEY of this book have been at the heart of
my work for years. You can see, as I have recounted experiences and
moments throughout my life thus far, how some of these thoughts,
ideas, and faith have taken shape.

I started to write this book, during a time my husband and I were
having some work done in our house. We live in an old but common

Victorian-style terraced house in middle England. Cracks everywhere, years of layers and layers of paint, old wallpaper, and quick-fix jobs done by previous owners. And while we decorated around it all, we were at a standstill until we could overhaul the walls and ceilings. So for two weeks, that's what we did, and, of course, it coincided with the beginning of the writing of this book. For the first few days, we had to vacate. There would have been too much dust and noise flying around to do anything. Then the next week and a half, we locked ourselves in the two upstairs bedrooms to do our respective work.

I brought our writing desk from the lounge to our bedroom upstairs and sat it in front of the window, and began to write. But before I did that, I decided that a few other projects had to be tempered to allow the creative time and headspace to write this book. I have created weekly pieces for my Patreon along the lines of post-Christian faith and thinking new thoughts. I put a tremendous amount of work into this each week. Readers deserve the best we can give them. Writing that is thoughtful, rich with resources, relatable, pastoral, and challenging. My husband urged me to invite them along on my book-writing journey. To press pause on the usual content and instead offer them a sneak peek into what I was writing, the process, and the personal journey that was about to be this book. I thought it was a great idea.

I sat down at my computer and wrote to my Patreon followers in a piece entitled, "Our little mess and dust everywhere." It was a reference to the literal state of our home at that moment, but as I began to write, it became clear to me just how fitting such a phrase was.

This is what post-Christianity feels like. We are standing in a bit of a mess; dust everywhere. Dust from the years of untouched possibility and dust from the rubble and ruins of the crumbling structures still continuing to avalanche. We are in a bit of a mess as we look around. But, also, philosophically, we are in a bit of a mess. The West was won atop traditional power structures of Christianity. How do we interpret life outside of it? We can't. The easy answer, as you have read, is secularism, but that is still a reaction to Christianity.

We can't exactly leave it in our dust because we are standing in the dust, and, of course, we are made of dust, so what is one to do?

Querying in this direction is what it means to engage post-Christian thought. I have been committed to this notion of post-Christianity for some time now and have been dedicated to putting out honest work towards this end for years. I hope I have done justice to this aim, but I'm not done and, by the nature of the task, never will be.

THEOLOGICAL PLASTICITY

In my first chapter, I opened with a scene from a pub in Belfast. I was sitting listening to a Radical Theologian speak of how we weren't done with the word god yet. He also spoke of plasticity, the plasticity of god. This was of particular interest to me as I had spent quite a bit of time for one of my Master's degrees studying neuroscience as it pertained to transformation. There is a concept known as the plasticity of the brain, by which we can heal our brains, growing new synapses with each new experience. By way of our social stimuli and environments, we can heal our brains one new story at a time as we build over the trauma-informed ones. This means our brains are plastic, not static. Which flies in the face of most of the neuroscience research of the 20th century. It is a life-changing discovery and filled with so much hope.

Robbins has done a lot with this idea of the plasticity of god. It has been extremely helpful in understanding new takes on what god might be and mean and how mechanisms of meaning-making, such as 'god' might continue in ways that make sense, speak to our humanity, and our own understanding of transformation. Robbins talks about the plasticity of god as it relates to the very core of the nature and reality of god and who and what we have come to know god as.

He takes his cues from the work of Catherine Malabou, who appropriated the concept of plasticity from breakthroughs in neuroscience over the last twenty years.

Malabou says, "Plasticity thus refers to the possibility of being transformed without being destroyed; it characterizes the entire strategy of modification that seeks to avoid the threat of destruction."[2] It is not that god is destroyed, but to use Malabou's words, a "metamorphosis" occurs. It is different, completely. But different unto itself and in relation to itself. God cannot become plastic as to change into a pen. But god is beautifully vulnerable to plasticity as it covers over dead and makes new, to be a better and truer form of itself.

We are talking about the changeability of god; no longer static, no longer lacking in motion, or modes of immobility and not even god as dead. But plastic. Talking about god in terms of theological plasticity says that god and god-consciousness are completely dynamic and change as we move forward into the future, and it is a conversation that bypasses being in the traditional sense of ontology. God and our god constructs are plastic enough to move from supernaturalism and metaphysicality into something else. We are not speaking in terms of 'elasticity' or 'flexibility.' Both these terms denote an original form which can always be returned to and by which the operation of movement is governed. Plasticity is a complete transformation from what was once, but as Malabou says, "never separating itself from itself."

Robbins says it like this,

> the radical theology I have in mind does not bespeak the nonexistence of God but rather the plasticity of God. The unconditional is not determined in the sense that it is fixed, but it is determined in the sense that it is plastic...God changes. The God who was, is no longer. Yet, still, we may see the God who is coming. [3]

The beauty of plasticity is that it isn't one change. As if God was *this*, but now god is *that*. It is the ever-honest process of death and change. Death by way of the death of god that acts as a crucible for the process of plasticity. Change by way of the living flow that is ever becoming, molding, and regeneration of god in our world, imminently.

It is still in service to the search for Other.

WHERE TO NOW?

So, what now? What do we do now in the name of us, our feet, and the direction they should be moving?

Mark Taylor had a similar question in the opening lines of his book that started to put Derrida on the theological map as it were, the question Derrida first asked and answered, "'We must begin *wherever we are...Wherever we are.*'" Taylor continues, "But where *are* we?"[4]

As you've read earlier, it seems easier for something to begin than to end. We are in a place now where we find we must simultaneously begin and end. We must begin *at* the end. But where and what is the end? And where, in fact, are we? Derrida and Taylor echo, *we are wherever we are.* Therefore, this is where we begin. At the end. Amid our little mess and dust everywhere, we begin.

Yet this moment is not necessarily a singular one. It is connected to all your moments leading up to this one and will be intricately and irrevocably connected to the next ones. Your experiences of faith are not simply relegated to categories of the sacred, divine, religion or even god. They are beholden, held, and loved by all of your life. Your dreams, sorrows, relationships, pains, and joys—all that sustains you and all that is you—is where you begin. Indeed, right where you left off. This is why I took the time to share so much of my story in chapter one. As Martin Hägglund writes,

> Even the greatest moments of happiness in love—gather-
> ing and deepening the qualitative experience of a shared
> life—cannot be contained in an instant, since the mo-
> ment is bound up with a network of meaning that ex-
> tends to the memory of a shared past and anticipations
> of a future together. As [Charles] Taylor himself empha-
> sizes: "The deepest, most powerful kind of happiness,
> even in the moment, is plunged into a sense of meaning,"
> so that "when you look back on your life together, those
> happy moments, those travels in the sun, were bathed in
> the awareness of other years, other travels, which seemed
> to come alive in the present one."[5]

We begin with all our happiness. We begin with our amazing, shared little lives in love and community. We begin with the sun shining on our faces or the cold rain beating down around us. We begin with the awareness of all our travels and all the travels yet to be had. All of it is present in this moment and the moments to come. We begin in the rubble, and the ruin of all that has been lost but which has not been forsaken. Rather it is embraced as plasticity occurs and we are led on in an unknown direction. With no guarantees, and no promises to be broken, we go forward in the direction of the unpromisable and risk all the comforts of certainty and our padded God in the sky for the chance to travel *safer than the known way; that shall be safer than Light.*

LOST CAUSE OR CAUSE FOR THE LOST?

There is a paradox to all of this, certainly. Many of them are obvious. However, a little less obvious, with an ache that comes from the tenderness of humble, weak truth, is the paradox of the lost cause. Because that is the elephant in the room, isn't it? The question that gnaws, that begs, that we try to escape with all our bad acts of oblivion. But in the spirit of being honest, as this whole book has strived to do and be, I turn to the words of Mark Taylor for the most audacious answer I have encountered to date, "Even if the cause is lost the pursuit is still just."[6] He makes this statement in the middle of delivering the grim forecast "of the problems we face," the "despair," and the fact that "obstacles do seem insuperable."[7]

This post-Christian journey has integrity, to say impossibility is possible. That even if all is lost, the pursuit of it all anyway is still worth it, for us and for the world. In the spirit of Jacques Derrida, John

Caputo says it like this: "you are really getting somewhere only when you are paralyzed and it is impossible to advance, only when there is no playable, programmable way to proceed."[8]

One of my favorite quotes of all time, theological or otherwise, one that I have used time and time again, and one that has been the inspiration for my faith and my life, was written by 20th-century theologian Schubert Ogden. When defining what it means to have faith, he simply states, "that life is worth the living of it."[9]

At the end of a book on post-Christian theology, I can unreservedly, wholeheartedly, and peacefully say that this is all the faith I need and all I desire. To live my life in a way where I have faith that it's all worth just the living of it. Because, indeed, it is! No matter the outcome, I lived in every way a person can, and someday I will die the same as everyone else. Irrespective of afterlife musings, content I will be to return to dust, knowing that I lived my life in service to its worth. That all pretense, veneer, and veil were pushed through, without cease, without fail but toward the finish, which, as you might have guessed, is unfinishable.

Traveling *safer than the known way* is a journey without end and a life and faith worth the living of it. This is it! Our religion, our Christianity, for better or for worse, has awoken us to our present faith. For all Christianity is and isn't, it has ultimately pointed in the direction of the whispers and the ghosts. To that little voice that says, 'Hey you! Life is worth the living of it! Your story matters, you matter, and the story that got you here matters too.'

I love religious imagery. Come into my house, and you will see antique pictures ranging from Dante's inferno, the fall of Lucifer from Paradise Lost, nuns, snake charmers, fortune tellers, serpents, angels, statues, and an array of saints and sinners. I love to be among it all.

I think I am particularly fascinated with what most religious people would qualify as grotesque, or at the very least undesirable to be hung in their home to see on a daily basis. Books I love to collect do not differ.

I think because of how I grew up, all the talk of the demonic and the darkness, all that was unseen lurking around to catch us in any slip-up. We were not to utter unholy words or think unholy thoughts. Certainly, we were not to have any unholy paraphernalia. All of this was a foothold for the devil and his friends. Obviously, being long free from that sort of obsessive, toxic, and fear-full thinking, I am now fascinated with such imagery as I am free to explore its interesting origins and the beautiful and glorious human hands in it all. All the meaning-making, and all the storytelling. The hopes and dreams of so many, and a vivid look at how various people have made sense of these things throughout time and history. I really do love it.

My husband bought me a book last year, *The Devil's Atlas: An Explorer's Guide to Heavens, Hells and Afterworlds* by Edward Brooke-Hitching. It is gorgeously colorful and each page is filled with images that span millennia of humanity's dealings and imagination when it comes to after-life calculations and speculations. The book is the result of ten years of research into old maps, discovered topographies, travels far and wide into archives, old book shops, village chronicles, literary allusions, historical documents, and more, all pointing to another world after this one. The book Brooke-Hitching has put together is stunning.

He talks about the attempts made through the ages to answer "the paradoxical challenge of these questions, with the certain knowledge that the answers are beyond human reach." He goes on to say, "This is a book about mapping the unmappable and painting the indescribable, to explore the unexplorable."[10]

While our answers will always be beyond human reach and perhaps beyond the reach of anything otherwise, it is welcome. Because we are mapping the unmappable and painting the indescribable as best we can. Because it is worth it, and our stories matter. All we have known and been, and all we are becoming. All that our faith is devolving and evolving into, all the lives and deaths our god(s) experience. All the haunting, the ghosting, the teasing, the taunting. All the disrupting and interrupting, the interrogating and erupting. Through it all, we can only be loyal to that which is Undeconstructible. This is perhaps what it means to be post-Christian. This is perhaps what it means to travel *safer than the known way*, toward what is next and what is to come.

"Amen. *Ite, missa est.* Go, it is ended, but I pray you, do not go in peace. Remember always to say 'perhaps.'"[11]

EPILOGUE

"If Satan has a bad reputation, it's because he has a thank-less job."[1]

— **Erik Butler**

ONE MORE QUESTION

ONE TIME WHEN I was little, I asked my mother a peculiar and curious question about prayer and forgiveness. I was in the backseat of the car, and she was upfront driving. I had endless questions, but ones that made sense to me to ask. I was told by a lot of Christians that I should be praying for the salvation of others because they could end up in hell. I was told that Jesus loved and died for everyone; there was no exception. But it would be too late by the time they died, and they had to choose him now. These things you could pray to happen. More than that, God wanted you to pray that they would. I did my best to pray for those close to me who I knew were not yet Christians that I very much wanted to be in heaven with me. I did this each night before bed.

The question that seemed logical was whether or not I should pray for the Devil to be saved. "Should I pray for the Devil? Should I pray that he finds Jesus? It must be possible that the Devil can receive forgiveness because Jesus died for everyone's sins, right?"

My mother told me that the Devil was not to be saved and that I shouldn't pray for him. I remember thinking, are we sure about this? Because everyone means everyone. But I was assured that day that I should stop praying for the Devil. So I did. I no longer prayed for the salvation of the Devil after that.

I mean, it seemed like a good idea. If the Devil got saved, we didn't have to worry about anything else. All the problems in the world would be solved. When I thought about the Devil, I felt bad for him. Maybe he regretted his decision. Maybe he wanted out. Maybe he was sorry for what he had done but didn't know how to undo it. He was mean and nasty and so hated. That can't feel good. I felt sad for him. I wanted him to follow Jesus like all of us and for all the evil in the world to go away. I wanted the Devil to be forgiven and saved.

A DEVILISH PRAYER

During the writing of this book, I read Nick Cave and Seán O'Hagan's *Faith, Hope and Carnage*, which they wrote during the pandemic. In the final chapter, Cave spoke with O'Hagan about how he had been working on a collection of Staffordshire-style figurines depicting the Devil's birth, life, and death. I have a thing for Victorian Staffordshire figurines, as well. I have several that I have been able to procure over the last few years, and I am very particular about the ones I own. My friends are puzzled as to why I have a peculiar appreciation for them. So, of course, I was very interested in Cave's attempt.

The 17-figure series portrays the Devil throughout various points of his life, including sailors corrupting him, killing of a child, going off to war, coming back from war, taking a bride, and his death. The final figurine in which his death is illustrated shows a ghost-like child reaching out to him in forgiveness. Somehow the Devil had been redeemed–forgiven.

I was immediately transported to that moment in the car with my mother as a little girl. Remembering how it felt to think about the evilness and corruption of the Devil and to feel sad for him, to desire that he experience forgiveness, too. I had all but forgotten this little memory until I read about Cave's Devil and his portrayal of forgiveness. I couldn't believe it. I had never heard anyone utter a word to this effect since I had posed that question to my mother so many years ago.

Part of being post-Christian is about telling new narratives. It's about smashing through all the theological sense we thought we were making, going as far as our imaginations can take us, and then going even further. There is a level of forgiveness that needs to be present as we continue to do this work that might deny long-held theological reason. I'm not sure what that all looks like yet. But perhaps we go as far as to forgive the Devil. Maybe the Devil *is* absolved. What if his rebellion was in loyalty to something other, and he refused to bow his knee where it was not due? Perhaps he was made corrupt by something in God's world, created by God, and it turned him. All we know is that beautiful Lucifer fell from grace and was never allowed a chance at forgiveness.

When we move post-Christian, it can often feel like a fall from grace. We are seen as enemies of Christianity, even though we are no such thing. We are labeled as lawless and weighed in as wayward, and that is the end of it. Yet, we are welcomed by all that is next. We experience a forgiveness in the darkness. We forgive ourselves, perhaps we forgive others, and maybe we even forgive our god(s). The Devil is forgiven for all he didn't do wrong, and we move forward full of faithful anticipation because it is all turned upside down now. What once was, is no more, and what is will be gone again. I want this. This is the life I prefer and dream of.

I would rather live a life praying for the Devil, keeping my heart open, hoping against hope than shutting out the possibility of the impossible. I wonder if 'praying' for our ghosts and goblins, demons and devils isn't part of what it means to be post-Christian and post-God? Not in the literal way we understand prayer and devils. But in a way that we now embrace everything we were told to resist. All those binary categories of good and evil, black and white, are quite a bit more blurred. Blurred because we are human, nuanced, and complex, and as long as we have breath there are always more chances and a fresh day.

We are post-Christian because not only does this apply to our devils but our god(s) as well. We pray for our god(s). As they change and transform, haunt and taunt. As they disappear and reappear, and as they die and come back to life. This is why we aren't atheist or agnostic. This is why Christianity still holds us and our stories in a lot of ways. This is precisely why we say post-Christian, as we are different, yet not completely separate from it.

I find this incredibly profound. Yet again another way to travel safer than what has been known.

So perhaps, if we do pray, may it be for anything that would haunt us, whispering of the world that is coming, that is here.

"Curiouser and curiouser..."

END NOTES

CHAPTER 1

1 Robbins, Jeffery. "Making Believe and Making a Mess: An Insurrectionist Theology." (lecture, Wake Festival, Belfast, Northern Ireland, April 25, 2017).

2 John D. Caputo, *Folly of God: A Theology of the Unconditional*. (Salem: Polebridge Press, 2015), 48.

3 N.T. Wright, *Simply Christian: Why Christianity Makes Sense*. (New York: Harper Collins, 2006), 8.

4 Ibid.

5 Ibid, 3.

6 Ibid, 3-4.

7 Caputo, *The Folly of God*, 30.

8 Ibid, 35.

9 Ibid, 34.

10 Nick Cave. *Introduction to The Gospel According to Mark: KJV Pocket Canons*. (Edinburgh: Canongate, 1998), xi.

11 Mark C. Taylor, *After God*. (Chicago: University of Chicago Press, 2007), acknowledgements.

12 Taylor, *After God*, introduction.

13 Robbins, "Making Believe and Making a Mess."

14 Caputo, *The Folly of God*, 28.

CHAPTER 2

1 Franco Berardi, *After the Future*, ed. Gary Genosko and Nicholas Thoburn. (Edinburgh: AK Press, 2011), 164.

2 Sex Pistols, "God Save the Queen," track 2 on *Never Mind the Bollocks*, recorded October 1976, Virgin.

3 Richard Kieckhefer, *Theology in Stone: Church Architecture from Byzantium to Berkeley*, (Oxford: Oxford University Press, 2004), 3.

4. Joeri Schrijvers and Martin Koci, ed., *The European Reception of John D. Caputo's Thought: Radicalizing Theology*. (London: Lexington Books, 2023)

5 Harvey Cox, *The Future of Faith*. (New York: Harper One, 2009), 213.

6 Mark C. Taylor, *About Religion: Economies of Faith in Virtual Culture*. (Chicago: The University of Chicago Press, 1999), 1.

7 "America's Changing Religious Landscape" Pew Research Center, May 12, 2015, https://www.pewforum.org/2015/05/12/americas-changing-religious-landscape/.

8 "Nones on the Rise" Pew Research Center, October 9, 2012, https://www.pewresearch.org/religion/2012/10/09/nones-on-the-rise/.

9 Barna Group and Impact 360 Institute, *Gen Z: The Culture, Beliefs and Motivations Shaping the Next Generation*. (Venture: Barna Group, 2018).

10 Ibid, 5.

11 "Modeling the Future of Religion in America" Pew Research Center, September 13, 2022, https://www.pewresearch.org/religion/2022/09/13/modeling-the-future-of-religion-in-ame

rica/.

12 Ibid.

13 Ibid.

14 Berardi, *After the Future*, 3.

15 Ibid, 6.

16 Greta Thunberg, "This Is All Wrong" (Speech present at the U.N. Climate Action Summit, New York City, NY, September 23, 2019).

17 Berardi, *After the Future*, 6

18 Ibid, 8.

19 Ibid.

20 Ibid, 12.

21 Graham Ward, *Theology and Religion: Why it Matters*. (Cambridge: Polity, 2019), 24.

22 Gianni Vattimo, *After Christianity*, trans. Luca D'Isanto. (New York: Columbia University Press, 2002), 1.

23 Ibid.

CHAPTER 3

1 John D. Caputo, *The Insistence of God: A Theology of Perhaps*. (Bloomington: Indiana University Press, 2013), 14.

2 Alain de Botton, *Religion for Atheists: A non-believer's guide to the uses of religion*. (London: Penguin Books, 2012), 11.

3 Jean-Luc Nancy, *Dis-Enclosure: The Deconstruction of Christianity*, Perspectives in Continental Philosophy, trans. by Bettina Bergo, Gabriel Malenfant, and Michael B. Smith (New York: Fordham University Press, 2008), 142.

4 Roger Haight, *Jesus: Symbol of God*. (Maryknoll: Orbis Books, 2000), 13.

5 Ibid.

6 Ibid, 14.

7 Ibid.

8 Ibid.

9 Ibid.

10 Ibid.

11 Ibid.

12 Ibid.

13 François Laurelle, *Clandestine Theology: A Non-Philosopher's Confession of Faith*, trans. Andrew Sackin-Poll. (London: Bloomsbury Academic, 2021), 95.

14 Ibid.

15 Ibid, viii.

16 J. L. Austin, *How to Do Things with Words: The William James Lectures Delivered at Harvard University in 1955*, ed. J.O. Ursom and Marina Sbisà. (Oxford: Oxford University Press, 1962).

17 Caputo, *The Insistence of God*, 14.

18 Ibid, 15.

19 Ibid.

CHAPTER 4

1 Barry Taylor, *Sex, God, and Rock'n'Roll: Catastrophes, Epiphanies, and Sacred Anarchies*. (Minneapolis: Fortress Press, 2020), 176.

2 John O'Donohue, *The Invisible Embrace of Beauty: Rediscovering the True Sources of Compassion*, Serenity, and Hope. (New York: Harper Collins, 2004), 31.

3 Friedrich Nietzsche, *The Gay Science: With a Prelude of Rhymes and an appendix of songs*, ed and trans.Walter Kaufmann, (New York: Vintage, 1974), 181-82.

4 Carl Raschke, *The New Reformation: Why Evangelicals Must Embrace Postmodernity*. (Grand Rapids: Baker Academic, 2004), 42.

5 Ibid.

6 Wilfred Cantwell Smith, *The Meaning and End of Religion*. (Minneapolis: Fortress Press, 1991), 135.

7 Ibid, 140

8 Raschke, *The New Reformation*, 47.

9 F. Leron Shults, *Theology After the Birth of God: Atheist Conceptions in Cognition and Culture*. (New York: Palgrave Macmillan, 2014), 3.

10 Ibid.

11 "Magazine covers that shook the world," Los Angeles Times, accessed September 1, 2021, https://www.latimes.com/entertainment/la-et-10magazinecovers14-july14-pg-photogallery.html.

12 "Bob Dylan: A Candid Conversation with the Visionary Whose Songs Changed the Times," interview by Ron Rosenbaum. *Playboy*, March 1, 1978.

13 Lily Rothman, "Is God Dead? At 50," TIME, March 2016, https://time.com/isgoddead/.

14 Ibid.

15 Thomas J.J. Altizer and William Hamilton, *Radical Theology and the Death of God*. (Indianapolis: The Bobbs-Merrill Company, Inc.:1966), 9.

16 Ibid.

17 Ibid.

18 Nietzsche, *The Gay Science*, Book III, Section 108.

19 Nathan Smith, "Thomas J.J. Alter and the Death of God," Nathan Smith Books (blog), May 21, 2019, https://www.nathansmithbooks.com/blog/2019/5/24/thomas-jj-altizer-and-the-death-of-god.

20 Altizer and Hamilton, *Radical Theology and the Death of God*, 10.

21 Thomas J.J. Altizer, Interview by Alec Gilmore. http://www.altizer.narod.ru/engtexts/interview.html, March 1968.

22 Caputo, *The Folly of God*, 1.

23 Ibid, 2.

24. Ibid.

25 Ibid, 35.

26 Slavoj Žižek, and John Milbank, ed. Creston Davis. *The Monstrosity of Christ: Paradox or Dialectic.* (Cambridge: MIT Press, 2011).

27 Hessert, Paul, *Christ and the End of Meaning: The Theology of Passion.* (Rockport: Element), 1993, 1

28 Ibid, xi.

29 John D. Caputo, *The Prayers and Tears of Jacques Derrida: Religion without Religion.* (Bloomington: Indiana University Press, 1997), 1.

30 Jeffrey Robbins, *Radical Theology: A Vision for Change.* (Bloomington: Indiana University Press, 2016), 5.

31 Ibid.

32 Ibid, 6.

33 John D. Caputo, *In Search of Radical Theology: Expositions, Explorations, Exhortations.* (New York: Fordham University Press, 2020), 4

34 Ibid.

35 Ibid.

CHAPTER 5

1 Caputo, *The Prayers and Tears of Jacques Derrida*, xxvii.

2 Martin Heidegger, *The Event*, trans. Richard Rojcewicz. (Bloomington: Indiana University Press), 2013), 217.

3 Caputo, *The Prayers and Tears of Jacques Derrida*, xviii.

4 Peter Salmon, *An Event, Perhaps: A Biography of Jacques Derrida.* (London: Verso, 2020), 2.

5 Ibid, 3.

6 Jean-Paul Martinon, *On Futurity: Malabou, Nancy & Derrida*. (Palgrave Macmillan, 2017), introduction.

7 Martinon, *On Futurity*, introduction.

8 Raschke, *The Next Reformation*, 13.

9 Caputo, *The Insistence of God*, 3.

10 Ibid, 5-7.

11 Ibid, 7.

12 Ibid, 3.

13 Keith Giles, ed., *Before you Lose Your Mind: Deconstructing Bad Theology in the Church*. (Oak Glen: Quoir, 2021).

14 John D. Caputo, *Deconstruction in a Nutshell: A Conversation with Jacques* Derrida. (New York: Fordham University Press, 1997), 74.

15 Vattimo, *After Christianity*, 6.

16 Julia Kristeva, *This Incredible Need to Believe*, trans. Beverly Bit Brahic. (New York: Columbia University Press, 2009), 1.

17 Ibid, 76.

18 Caputo, *The Prayers and Tears of Jacques* Derrida, 3.

19 Ibid, 5.

20 Ibid.

21 Caputo, *The Insistence of God*, 3.

CHAPTER 6

1 Richard Kearney, *Anatheism: Returning to God After God*, (New York: Columbia University Press, 2011), 5.

2 Ibid, 3.

3 Ibid, xiv.

4 Ibid.

5 Ibid.

6 Ibid, xv.

7 Ibid, 3.

8 Ibid, 17.

9 Ibid, 21.

10 Ibid, 25.

11 Caputo, *The Folly of God*, 2.

12 B. Keith Putt, ed., *The Essential Caputo: Selected Writings*. (Bloomington: Indiana University Press, 2018), 49.

13 Ibid.

14 Ibid, 49-50.

15 Ibid, 234.

16 Caputo, *Deconstruction in a Nutshell*, 52.

17 Gordon D. Kaufman, *In the beginning...Creativity*. (Minneapolis: Fortress Press, 2004), 73.

CHAPTER 7

1 Mark C. Taylor, *Abiding Grace: Time, Modernity, Death*. (Chicago: The University of Chicago Press, 2018), 2.

2 Raschke, *The Next Reformation*, 211.

3 Taylor, *Abiding Grace*, 2.

4 Dave Tomlinson, *The Post-Evangelical: SPCK Classic – with a New Preface*. (London: SPCK Publishing, 2014), preface.

5 Mary Ruti, *A World of Fragile Things: Psychoanalysis and the Art of Living*. (Albany: State University of New York, 2008), introduction.

6 Carter Heyward, *Saving Jesus from Those Who Are Right: Rethinking What It Means to Be Christian*. (Minneapolis: Fortress Press, 1999), preface.

7 Ibid, 2.

8 Ibid, 8.

CHAPTER 8

1 Heidegger, *The Event*, 219.

2 Raschke, *The Next Reformation*, 53.

3 Ibid.

4 Ibid.

5 John D. Caputo, *The Weakness of God: A Theology of Event*. (Bloomington: Indiana University Press, 2006), 13.

6 Ibid.

7 Ibid.

8 Ibid, 14.

9 Ibid.

10 Ibid.

CHAPTER 9

1 Catherine Malabou, Interview by Kjetil Horn Hogstad. "Plasticity and Education - An interview with Catherine Malabou," June 15 2021.

https://www.tandfonline.com/doi/full/10.1080/00131857.2021.1940140.

2 Catherine Malabou, *Ontology of the Accident: An Essay on Destructive Plasticity*, trans. Carolyn Shread. (Cambridge; Polity Press, 2012), 44-45.

3 Robbins, *Radical Theology*, 159.

4 Taylor, *Erring*, 3.

5 Martin Hägglund, *This Life: Secular Faith and Spiritual Freedom*. (New York: Pantheon Books, 2019), 59.

6 Taylor, *After God*, xviii.

7 Ibid.

8 Caputo, *The Prayers and Tears of Jacques Derrida*, xxvii.

9 Schubert M. Ogden, *On Theology*. (Dallas: Southern University Press, 1986), 106.

10 Edward Brooke-Hitching, *The Devil's Atlas: An Explorer's Guide to Heavens, Hells and Afterworlds*. (London: Simon and Schuster, 2022), 10.

11 Caputo, *The Insistence of God*, 23.

EPILOGUE

1 Erik Butler, T*he Devil and his Advocates*. (London: Reaction Books, 2021), introduction.